T0209735

# THE FOURTH BRAIN:
## A Different Way of Living

### Beyond Emotional Intelligence

GINA BRIBANY

**BALBOA.**
PRESS

A DIVISION OF HAY HOUSE

Balboa Press books may be ordered through booksellers or by contacting:

Balboa Press
A Division of Hay House
1663 Liberty Drive
Bloomington, IN 47403
www.balboapress.com
1 (877) 407-4847

Because of the dynamic nature of the Internet, any web addresses or
links contained in this book may have changed since publication and
may no longer be valid. The views expressed in this work are solely those
of the author and do not necessarily reflect the views of the publisher,
and the publisher hereby disclaims any responsibility for them.

The author of this book does not dispense medical advice or prescribe the use
of any technique as a form of treatment for physical, emotional, or medical
problems without the advice of a physician, either directly or indirectly. The
intent of the author is only to offer information of a general nature to help
you in your quest for emotional and spiritual well-being. In the event you use
any of the information in this book for yourself, which is your constitutional
right, the author and the publisher assume no responsibility for your actions.

Any people depicted in stock imagery provided by Getty Images are
models, and such images are being used for illustrative purposes only.
Certain stock imagery © Getty Images.

Print information available on the last page.

ISBN: 978-1-9822-2094-5 (sc)
ISBN: 978-1-9822-2095-2 (e)

Balboa Press rev. date: 02/20/2019

# CONTENTS

# ACKNOWLEDGEMENT
# FROM THE AUTHOR

*Without the experiences and support from my family,*
*friends, and colleagues, this book would not exist.*
*Thanks to my mother and father for bringing me to life*
*Thanks to my sister Dalia and my brother Jhon for teaching*
*me the importance of living in the present moment.*
*Thanks to Victoria Rueda for her support and encouragement.*
*Thanks to Kevin Panameno for teaching me*
*the importance of unlearning to evolve.*
*Thanks to my clients who allow me to*
*use their stories for the book.*
*Thanks to Jhon Cardona for helping me with*
*the English translation of the book.*
*Thanks to Christine Williams and Doug Tuthill for reading*
*my drafts and help me with the English grammar.*
*To all the individuals I have had the opportunity*
*to learn from, I want to say thank you for being the*
*inspiration for The Original Intelligence Model.*
*Thanks, more please.*

# INTRODUCTION

*The vision will only come when one can look at one's heart. The one who looks outside dreams, the one who looks inside wakes up. Carl Jung*

To have knowledge about something new and innovative doesn't make us smarter. Being smart is not simply about our ability to consciously choose the best options to achieve the best results. Unlike what people previously thought, intelligence does not necessarily have to respond to common sense because there are other kinds of logic that we have not finished discovering or understanding. If we just follow what is known, innovation would disappear.

Depending on what kind of intelligence we are talking about, intelligence is knowing what to do at a certain time to obtain what we need. Conversely, to stand aside, to allow things to flow, and to stop believing that we must control everything is another form of intelligence.

There are cognitive mechanisms for achieving temporary results, but that's not my focus. For example, we could use a rational strategy to obtain a new house, car, or job, believing that the house or car will bring us greater happiness, and a new job we will help us end interpersonal problems.

But having the intelligence to get a house, car, or new job is not the intelligence to acquire what we truly need, which is to grow emotionally and overcome conflicts so we can feel happy and complete. This is why we change jobs but continue to have the same type of boss, and we change partners but continue to attract the same type of conflict.

This book is an invitation to live coherently, inducing the awakening of a new level of consciousness that rises through the practice of certain biological and energetic principles which regulate our interaction with the internal and external world. This book will guide you to know about the four brains we possess and how they bring awareness to our potential for choice and creation. By learning when and how to activate these brains, you will be able to develop a new intelligence and way of life.

You are about to discover an intelligence that transcends the limitations of personality, ego, and body, and goes beyond emotional intelligence. This intelligence is emerging from the fourth brain that has been discovered by Dr. John A. Armour, "The brain of the heart."

The human heart begins to beat before the brain develops and long before the whole fetus is formed. Previously, we wondered what caused the beating and where the intelligence came from to start and regulate the heartbeat of a small being who was just starting to form. Recently, science has discovered that the heart has its own brain and intelligence, and it sends more signals to the brain in the head than it receives.

The heart is our first brain, but not the most rudimentary because unlike the other three, the heart brain possesses a cosmic, universal, original intelligence that goes beyond our current understanding.

As humans, we have needs, aspirations, dreams, and nightmares. Although for many it is hard to accept, we are the makers of our own destiny. To develop this new intelligence, we must gain awareness and recognize that the choices we make correspond to our conscious or unconscious needs. As Carlos Gustavo Jung said:

*"Those who do not learn anything from the unpleasant facts of their lives, force the cosmic consciousness to reproduce them as many times as necessary to learn what the drama of what happened teaches. What you deny you submit; what you accept transforms you."*

Maslow's hierarchy of needs provides us with an important starting point. We have five needs or motivators which go in the following ascending order: basic or physiological needs, the needs of security and protection, the needs of affiliation or affection, the needs of recognition, and finally the need for realization. Maslow said we all aim to meet these needs. However, when the immediate previous need has not been satisfied to a certain level, the following becomes more challenging to reach. We cannot focus our attention and effort on the next one unless we have been able to meet the previous need. We can all be stuck in one or more of these basic or survival necessities and not be aware. Consequently, we can have problems being intimate and establishing harmonious relationships, to satisfy recognition, trust, success, and self-realization, which are a constant life challenge because these are superior needs.

Although, according to Maslow, we all have these needs, their hierarchy is not static and can vary depending on the culture, education, beliefs, and the value system of each individual or family clan. Just as happiness is subjective and independent of cultural needs and stereotypes, self-realization is still possible even when material or basic deficiencies exist if there are spiritual motivators or coherence and connections that transcend the personal. That is to say, a consciousness of transpersonal order.

In experiments with people who won the lottery and others who were imprisoned, the researchers determined that after a year these people reached the same level of happiness they had before winning the lottery or having been incarcerated. This happens because we tend to fall into our predetermined level of happiness regardless of our circumstances. What makes us happy ends up being another belief.

While physiological needs are innate to us, other needs are built from our interaction with family, culture, and society. We can also inherit a need or believe we have one by recognizing the need and where it comes from. We can cut those connections and ties that keep us united to those created or inherited needs. These needs can also be called mental programs, which could be inherited from generation to generation.

Our work here is to identify which needs we are stuck on and where they come from or were generated. As soon as we understand this, we satisfy them or stop believing in them and demystify them. Once satisfied, the needs cease to act as motivators and the pattern of behavior changes as well as our unconscious thoughts and all that it brings.

Remember, it is unmet needs which generate unwanted behavior. Depending on the need in which we are anchored, we use a specific type of brain to satisfy that need. Usually the result is a placebo that makes you feel you have reached something, when in reality we perpetuate the same need because of not knowing what we really are looking for through every attitude and action we make. Every brain has its own intelligence and results.

Let's begin our exploration of the four brains and their four ways of living. But first, I want to ask a question: Have I created the need to read what comes next?

# CHAPTER 1

# THE FOUR BRAINS AND
# THEIR LIFE STYLE

In each of us there are three different forces that coexist: one that thinks, another that feels, and one more that we are. These are the root of coherence and happiness in humans. As Mahatma Gandhi said, *"Happiness is when what you think, what you say, and what you do are in harmony."* The first three brains are part of what we think and what we feel, while the fourth brain is part of who we are.

The American neuroscientist Paul MacLean proposed in 1970 "the triple brain hypothesis," in which he explained we had three brains instead of one. The description of these three brains, their evolution, and their functioning will help us understand the first three ways of living life.

**In the nucleus is where we can find the most primitive brain of the three. The Reptilian Brain**, which is responsible for controlling the most vital functions of the body such as breathing, body temperature, and balance. It is called reptilian because it possesses the same structures found in the brain of reptiles: the brain stem and the cerebellum. This brain is what reflects our four most basic motivating or instinctive behaviors

1

of survival, known as the four F's: fighting, fleeing, feeding, and fucking.

According to my analysis, the reptilian lifestyle is rigid, basic, and compulsive. The reptilian personality seeks survival and satisfying the most basic needs. Generally, these people act from one or more of these four motivators that are activated by traumatic or unresolved childhood experiences because they had felt at risk, unprotected, abandoned, or rejected.

Some extreme examples of reptilian attitudes are: war, paranoia, xenophobia, fanaticism, narcissism, racism, classism, violence, and discrimination.

The most common examples of reptilian attitudes that are more socially accepted and into which we all fall without being aware are generalization, value judgments, defensiveness, manipulation, anger, raising the tone of voice, lying, controlling, and pretending. On its more positive side, the reptilian personality could be identified in those people who we consider conformists. They are happy just having food and a roof over their heads. They do not possess aspirations nor dreams. They just survive the day to day.

The reptilian brain regulates the involuntary physiological functions of our body and is responsible for the most primitive part of reflex response. It does not think or feel emotions. It only acts when our body asks for a reaction, such as hormones and temperature control, hunger, thirst, reproductive motivation, and respiration.

**Above the reptilian, we have the second brain, the limbic brain**, which stores our emotions and memories. Inside is the amygdala, considered the basis of affective memory. Among the functions and motivations of the limbic brain are fear, anger, the love of our parents, social relations, and jealousy. The limbic lifestyle is intense, sensitive, and even dramatic. Everything can affect a person with a negative limbic personality. They could take everything as a personal matter, could be spiteful, nervous, undecided, depressive, and anxious because they frequently feel attacked by their surroundings or others. On the positive side, we can also find emotionally sensitive people who feel empathy and easily connect with the emotions of others, but if they stay attached to this brain they will not be able to transcend the emotionality. They burnout easily.

**We have the third brain, the neocortex** or rational brain, which allows us to be conscious and capable of controlling emotions. It also develops cognitive capacities such as memorization, concentration, self-reflection, problem solving, and the skill to choose the right behavior. It is the conscious part of the person, both physiologically and emotionally. A person with rational personality is calculating, wants to find rational explanations to everything he or she sees or experiences, can be skeptical, pragmatic, repress his/her emotions, abhor drama, and, when pushed over the edge, can be insensitive or short of empathy. The rational personality only addresses secondary or social emotions; it hardly could get to the primary emotions or unmet needs.

Some of the responsibility for achieving a comprehensive state of health relies on the structure called the limbic brain amygdala, which conditions our executive systems and emotional self-control of the neocortex (rational), while conditioning our physical health (reptilian). When stress seizes us, the amygdala is activated, does not work normally, and this alteration causes the brain to inadequately process the sensory information that comes mainly through hearing, and from other senses. This is when we react with impulsiveness and block the functions of the neocortex or rational brain, including the ability to solve problems and have emotional self-control, which negatively influences our wellbeing and our performance and interpersonal relationships.

Although those four instincts of fighting, fleeing, feeding and sexuality, mentioned previously, are part of our human nature, evolution has created new and more sophisticated motivators that respond to today's world. However, we can all activate these instincts in the face of extreme circumstances. The challenge is to activate and deactivate them and not allow them to become our lifestyle. Our interpretation of reality plays a decisive role. We assign value and meaning to the things that happen to us and that meaning is a continuous decision that determines which of our instincts or motivators will be activated, resulting in a series of behaviors and attitudes from physiological to psychological.

These three brains or brain of the head has an extended neuronal connection to the gut. There are hundreds of million of neurons connecting the brain to the enteric nervous system, the part of the nervous system that is in charge of controlling the gastrointestinal system. The trillions of microbes residing in the gut are listened and the gut movements and sensations communicate to this brain our stage of physical health.

**The fourth brain is the brain of the heart.** Canadian neurologist Dr. Andrew Amour discovered a sophisticated collection of neurons in the heart, organized with a complex independent nervous system that has about 40,000 neurons called sensory neurites that communicate with the brain of the head. 400 times more than, the brain sends out to the rest of the body. Later, I will explain in greater detail the characteristics of the heart brain, but for now I will focus on describing its personality.

The heart personality is compassionate, loving, breathes in harmony, feels part of a whole, does not blame but seeks alternatives and solutions, looks for the positive side of things, is optimistic, cheerful and cooperative, takes responsibility for its actions and is connected with its inner self and its purpose in life, and expresses it easily. These personalities are sincere, respectful and do not resist challenges. They flow during challenging situations. They are stable and enjoy self-confidence.

## The Origin Of Emotions

If you were on an ecological excursion in a rainforest and suddenly a panther started moving towards you, what would you do? Your instinct of survival would surely say you are in danger, that you have to run away, instinctively and without noticing the blood of your body concentrating on your legs and arms with the intention of getting prepared for running or facing the animal. The amygdala enters a state of emergency by identifying the danger and in just seconds changes all our physiology to preserve our physical integrity. Our arms and legs acquire abnormal levels of strength and speed in order to run, jump, and fight in unusual ways, but always to keep alive. Feeling the fear, the amygdala is then responsible for sending elevated levels of blood, oxygen, adrenaline, and glucose to certain parts of our body. The organs less involved in this act of survival will send the blood to those who need it. Our mouth and stomach, for example, will remain with low blood pressure, as well as the reproductive organs, because at this critical moment of emergency, we do not think about eating or reproducing. We only react to survive the predator.

Neurology has found that the first cerebral region through which sensory signals from the eyes or ears pass is the thalamus, which is responsible for distributing the messages to the other regions of the brain. Once there, the signals are directed to the neocortex, where the information is weighted by different levels of cerebral circuits to have a complete notion of what is happening and finally to emit a response according to the situation. The neocortex analyzes the situation and turns to the prefrontal lobes to understand and organize the stimuli to offer an analytical and proportionate response. It then sends those signals to the limbic system where the amygdala produces the required hormonal responses.

Although this is how our brain works most of the time, Joseph LeDoux discovered that there is a small neural structure, or shortcut, which directly communicates the thalamus with the amygdala. This short pathway allows the amygdala to receive some signals straight from the senses and triggers a hormonal secretion that determines our behavior before those signs have been recorded by the neocortex, which is extremely beneficial in case of being attacked by a predator.

However, this survival mechanism is not only triggered by predators or a threat to our physical integrity. Imagine that person at work who makes you feel threatened, humiliated, underrated and/or attacked is coming towards you. Your survival instinct would be triggered and the amygdala in the brain would send signals to the rest of the body to get defensive before the interaction begins. You may feel a slight pressure in your stomach and your face will be ready to disguise what you truly feel.

This survival mechanism, although beneficial in most cases, can generate side effects when the state of emergency is not overcome. When we feel threatened or attacked, which is part of the limbic lifestyle, a constant and sustained survival response of the amygdala can develop what is known as amygdala hijack, in which we experience difficulties thinking clearly, making decisions efficiently, and memorizing or learning new things. This is most commonly known as post-traumatic stress or continuous stress. When we are subjected to this type of stress, when we do not feel valued or appreciated, and instead we feel threatened, afraid of losing our job, fearful of ending a relationship, or that our public image is affected, we begin to experience the physiological response of the sustained amygdala. This manifest itself in many health disorders, such as gastro duodenal ulcers, indigestion, colitis, skin allergies, colds, and infections because our defense system decreases noticeably. How would it not if it is working twenty-four hours to protect us from a threat.

We can also suffer an "amygdala hijack" when we lose someone or something, which generates a period of mourning. At some point in our lives we all experience the loss of a loved one, a job, a place or a valuable object such as a property. This process, although painful, can eventually be overcome. However, at the beginning, the loss can generate an excess of cortisol due to the state of shock and stress. We resist accepting what is happening, we feel dazed, we go through anger, guilt, nervousness, or fear, and we can experience discouragement, loss of motivation, lethargy, sadness, and anxiety. This is because the hormone called "dopamine", that is responsible for maintaining our motivation, encouragement, and happiness, decreases to its lowest levels during this "hijack." Our body goes through an imbalance and the impact it generates varies depending on how important that loss is to us.

The other problem is that the amygdala offers immediate answers that do not consider the situational context. Instead, it is limited to associating social or interpersonal situations with the emotional memories that are stored and provides exaggerated responses that were previously used when threatened by a predator, when what is happening is we are just having a conversation with our mother-in-law.

## Our Adaptation Mechanism

Imagine you are forced to live in a foreign country with language, customs, laws, climate, and food you do not know. How would you feel? It might sound like an adventure, but it would surely generate uncertainty.

Our adaptive mechanism, unlike the survival mechanism, is triggered when we face change and uncertainty. When we experience a traumatic event or when our physical or psychological integrity is threatened, the survival mechanism is activated. But when we face change and the unknown and uncertainties that come with that change, the adaptation mechanism activates. This adaptation mechanism was developed because of drastic changes in nature such as food loss or scarcity, or the dryness of the land that caused us to change our nutrition and become carnivorous. So, we adapt to climate changes and other environmental circumstances. The funny thing is that although the times and our environment have changed, we continue to use the same mechanisms of survival and adaptation for unknown situations that we have not been through before. But because they are new and generate uncertainty we feel threatened and act like animals. We are territorial. We mark territories with words. We intimidate others, we fight to gain power and we are part of tribes to which we are faithful because we fear being banished and living the fate of our ancestors, who were easy prey for predators when they were alone. All of this is working unconsciously and impacts our daily behavior.

Each mechanism has a different purpose. One helps us survive, the other to adapt. Sometimes we make the mistake of using the wrong mechanism or right one in excess. If we were able to activate the survival mechanism in the face of change, it would be impossible to adapt. Running, fleeing, defending ourselves or being paralyzed could be useful in front of predators, but it has an adverse effect on change. This is what makes us stay still, feel overwhelmed, and stressed. Therefore, we cannot make decisions efficiently because adjustment is so threatening that we feel at risk and go into a survival mode. On the other hand, if we use creativity, introspection, and time to explore and make decisions, which are characteristic of the adaptation mechanism, in front of a predator, we would quickly be the Christmas dinner of other species.

The adaptation mechanism is radically different from the survival one. It requires developing new mental capacities to overcome challenges and improve processes that facilitate environmental. This implies that we develop high levels of attention to be able to observe with greater clarity and precision what is happening around us. Awareness and attention develop creativity and our ability to generate new resources and optimize those we already have. It is fortuitous that life has innumerable challenges for our species because that is what keeps us alert, motivated, and excited about what we can become. Hence, the importance of aspirations because not having them makes our life senseless. We need challenges to keep us curious and inspire us to move forward. So, if you don't have one yet, start building it.

The adaptation mechanism in the cerebral cortex strengthens this part of the brain as we use it. These neural connections increase our concentration to improve our analytical capacity and creativity. Neurons in the hippocampus are keys to controlling the amygdala so that it is not overactive in the uncertainty of change. The Amygdala activation would easily lead us into a state of panic and blockage, which is what commonly happens when we choose the wrong mechanism when we are in danger without understanding there is an opportunity to grow. When we don't accept our circumstances when we resist change and look at our reality with negativity. We automatically activate the survival mechanism and that is when someone ask "How are you?" The immediate response is "surviving," because you are. But remember, we can always choose what kind of experiences we will have. Something I will explain later.

With these biological conditions, it is not surprising that when we suffer a strong trauma after being abandoned, not recognized, subjected to hostile environments and family insecurity, or abused, we show a disproportionate reaction when we face a similar scenario or when we are in front of someone who reminds us, in some way, of the aggressor.

Imagine how much this can condition our emotional intelligence if most of our intense emotional memories, which are stored in the amygdala, come from the first years of life, from situations we could not control and are part of our unconscious memories. In the child's mind, there are more neural connections than in the adult's. This is because in the first five years of life the child stores huge amounts of energy and information from every interaction he or she has with the environment or persons around her. Everything is recorded, interpreted, and stored, from a minimum eye contact or a hug to indifference and lack of physical or verbal contact. For this reason, it is important to talk to children and explain to them family events, so they do not make conjectures or draw incorrect conclusions. Silence and family secrets create chains of programs that are inherited with awful consequences. We believe that by hiding family incidents and unwanted or shameful stories we are protecting the child from learning them, when in reality we are perpetuating those memories in our family tree, generation after generation, because the child receives information through his observation and perception of the environment and develops mental programs which can be unconscious limitations.

Awareness, acceptance, and resignification of challenges are opportunities to grow and advance, allowing us to find new ways and alternatives to succeed. If we focus our attention on not being attacked, not being hurt, not being deceived or not failing. If we focus on what we DO NOT want to happen and avoid it at all costs, our survival mechanism activates and makes us hostile. It decreases our social interaction capacities, we lose energy, and we are left alone and bitter. Instead, when we focus on what we want to achieve, what we want to happen, our biochemistry changes as well as our mental capacities and mood so that we can overcome day to day obstacles and challenges. We obtain better results and our life changes positively.

I want to emphasize that I am not simply speaking from a positivist discourse. Studies of neurology have found that when we hold a negative internal dialogue in which we say things such as," I will not be able, I am lost, I can never overcome it, it is too much for me, and I cannot handle this anymore," this negative dialogue activates the same parts of the brain that are activated when we feel we are about to die. This triggers the parts of the brain responsible for creativity, problem solving, analytical and recursive capacity that do not receive enough blood supply. In other words, when we cultivate negative thoughts we block our ability to solve challenges and difficulties, we reject our ability to see things as they are because we are thinking about what can happen in the worst case scenario.

Dr. Bandura, professor of psychology at Stanford University, showed that when confidence is conveyed in the capacity that we and others have, when coping with challenges and difficulties, a series of hormones called Neuropeptides are released in the blood. These hormones are able to inhibit the amygdala so that it does not activate. It does not block our mind, allowing us to think clearly and logically to make better decisions.

This self-confidence is an intelligence that allows us to expect the best. If we are optimistic and confident in our abilities and those of others to solve any circumstances, we will be creating an environment for our mental intelligence to respond positively. Fear may appear. It is not about avoiding fear. It is about leaving fear alone and focusing on our strengths. Then fear will starve and disappear when we are confident.

# CHAPTER 2

# CREATING COHERENCE

In both situations described above, our instinct of survival or adaptation works through our experiences and those of our ancestors, which have been recorded and incorporated into our mind. These are remembered and activated by similar experiences and our interpretations and emotions that accompany them.

When we make decisions, our feelings count as much or more than our rational thought. This was the case of Charles Darwin, the father of the theory of evolution, who at the age of 28 asked himself whether he should marry or devote himself exclusively to his research. Darwin had such an analytical mind that he took a sheet of paper, which is still preserved, marked out two columns and on the left he wrote all the arguments in favor of marriage, and on the right side he wrote all the reasons against marriage. His reasons against marriage were: "not having freedom to go wherever he pleased," "less time to meet with smart men in the club," "to have more expenses and the anxiety of the children," "not being able to read in the evenings," and "less money for books." His reasons for marriage were "children" and "constant companionship and friendship in old age." After analyzing the pros and cons,

Darwin finally concluded it was better to stay single and devote his life to investigation.

What Darwin did not know was that the heart was smarter than his brain and it would cause him to change his mind as soon as he met Emma Wedgewood, his cousin, with whom he fell in love. Emma became the love of his life and they had 10 children. Although Darwin had made a rational decision not to get married and remain single, one of the four brains made decisions for him beyond rationality, through intuition and love.

Darwin's situation is an example of how the decisions we make are not ruled solely by logic and reason. Our decisions are first intuitive and then we rationalize and justify them, even if we think otherwise. Paradoxically, a man's intelligence is not commonly valued by his intuitions but by his reasoning. Intuitions are shortcuts that our brains use to make faster decisions.

In the book, "The Righteous Mind: Why Good People Are Divided by Politics and Religion," Jonathan Haidt argues that intuition happens first and reasoning comes later. Haidt supports this idea with multiple social experiments using the same scenarios with different ethnic groups. He demonstrated that peoples' judgments are largely determined by their beliefs, ideologies, culture, and social group. His studies also show that once we take sides or adopt an ideology, we become blind to other arguments and seek to justify what we have decided. We defend the group we belong to, our tribe, because it guarantees security, membership, status, and other social needs. This is how we become irrational, allowing our survival instincts to control our actions.

A big step towards the development of a new intelligence is to be aware that the world we see is not real. What we observe, hear, and perceive is not real because it is filtered and interpreted through our senses. We must be aware that our emotions only respond to our interpretation of reality. There are times when we are at a dead end, convinced of being in a problem and without any good options. This happens because our brains deceive us and create emotions from stories that weave in the presence of threatening or seductive elements. Our mind assumes things, interprets unfinished fragments the information and draws conclusions quickly to confirm the history we have created. It projects our future by filling the missing data with information from the present and it is so insistent we end up believing it.

To be successful we need to acquire internal coherence, which is not so much about saying the right thing to the right person, at the right time, in the right way, but rather making sure that what we think, feel, say, and do are in coherence. Coherence not is training ourselves to control our emotions and thoughts to express something more appropriately and respectfully. It is to transcend the immediate emotion, and judgments so we can let go what we truly think and feel. For example, if you transcend the secondary emotion of not feeling recognized, you can discover the primary emotion of not feeling good enough, and at that time you could take responsibility for what happens to you and stop projecting it externally by being the victim.

Reality is designed in our brains. Everything is shaped in there. Spaces, smells, cold, warmth, people, distance, sadness, joy... everything is in our head. The outside could be different from what we perceive. The world is only within us. The conditions are the same, but subjectivity is different. Any negative or positive experience, more or less intense, is ultimately a subjective interpretation. Therefore, the more self-consciousness we have the less we will have to control or manage.

## Understanding Our Own Emotions

Towards the end of the nineteenth century Charles Darwin, William James, and Sigmund Freud wrote extensively about the different aspects of emotion, giving it a privileged place in scientific discourse. For most of the twentieth century, the laboratory distrusted emotion. It was said to be too subjective, elusive, and vague. It was judged to be antagonistic to reason, which was thought to be independent of and superior to emotion. Twentieth-century science dodged the body and moved emotion to the brain, but relegated it to the lower neural levels, associated with ancestors that no one respected. At that time, not only were emotions considered irrational, but even studying emotions was often seen as irrational. It took many years for cognitive and neuro science to accept emotion as equally important to logic.

Scientific has now confirmed the interdependency of emotions and cognition. The psychologist and specialist in neuroscience and human development, Mary Helen Immordino-Yang, who studied the physiological, psychological, and neuronal bases of emotions, self-awareness, and culture, says that emotions are essential in decision making because they have a primary component to determine if the situation implies a risk or danger. She argues that the selective reduction of emotion will make our decisions much worse and backs it up with studies of patients who had brain-damage in areas where emotions were dissociated from decision making, which led the patients to have psychotic disorders, significantly damaging their ability to make good decisions. Therefore, the goal is not to suppress or control our emotions, but to welcome them with an attitude of observation, trying to understand their cause and being attentive to the flow of emotions as we are experiencing them to understand their origin and be able to make more coherent decisions by our true self.

Neurological evidence shows that the absence of emotions is a problem. Emotions are intimately related to stability and coherence when it comes to making decisions. Reason is the "secretary" of intuitions and emotions because reason only makes final edits to make sure decisions makes sense. *"It is literally neurobiologically impossible to build memories, have complex thoughts or make meaningful decisions without emotion.... we just think about what we care for."* Mary Helen Immordino-Yang, from her book, Emotions, Learning and the Brain (p. 8).

Emotions, from a biological perspective, exist to helps us survive. In the beginning, we acquired the capacity to retain and preserve basic visual representations of our surroundings and gradually our mind started recording a flood of images which would later become specific scenarios. Then we classify them giving priority to certain scenarios, according to practicality. The more they recurred in our daily lives, the more easily we remembered them and the more they were involved with our survival as a species. This differentiate us from animals because we learned soon that we could survive by comparing, differentiating, and choosing what to do in each scenario, without having to drastically modify our physical body as other species do.

That was how we got to increase our brain volume. We stored more and more life experiences until we reached a point in which we discovered a shortcut. We realized that in some situations we did not need to decide, but simply act. This shortcut made it possible for us to act instead of thinking or comparing whenever we are in front of a wild animal or when we face an imminent danger. Our body developed the nervous system and stored these scenarios in our unconscious in such a way that these decisions became our instincts, reflexes, and emotions.

Here is when our five basic emotions and objectives are set according to Gestal psychology: MATEA (in Spanish)

- Fear: Its objective is protection and care.
- Affection: Its objective is association and connection.
- Sadness: Its goal is to make you get away. When we feel sad our body is telling us to "get away from there and go back to be with yourself."
- Anger: its objective is defense.
- Joy: Its objective is enlivening. It is the battery of our existence.

If you list these emotions from one to five according to their difficulty for you to experience, (e.g., 1 less difficult and 5 more difficult to experience), you will find the areas where you must work.

Example:

F (Fear) 1
A (Affection) 2
S (Sadness) 4
A (Anger) 3
J (Joy) 5

The emotions you mark with 4 and 5 are the areas to emphasize because they would mean the following:

F (Fear) I have trouble protecting myself.
A (Affection) I have a hard time connecting.
S (Sadness) I have trouble being by myself.

A (Anger) I have trouble putting limits.
J (Joy) I find it hard to get energy and vitality.

There is an instinctive unconscious force of thousands of years influencing our behavior. Our challenge is to become aware that we can face certain scenarios in more creative and intelligent ways, decode some automatic responses, understand that we are immerse in new scenarios which are constantly changing. But more importantly, we can comprehend that we are the ones who create these settings and that we need a new model of interaction with our surroundings. We need a less reactive and more proactive model, one that does not seek competition but collaboration, that does not seek individualization but integration. One where I become aware that what happens to others has to do with me, where we recognize union instead of only separation.

Here are two stories that clearly exemplify how our early experiences and history can condition us to limit our self-realization when we are not aware of them.

Three years ago, I started therapy work with Karla, a young woman who wanted to find more stability in her relationships. Karla was without her mom since she was nine years old. Her mother was ran over by a car. Karla did not talk about this with anyone, not even with her family. She did discuss her mom's death with two trusted friends. This was an unresolved struggle for her and, as our conversations advanced, she made it clear that she was laying all her trust in me, which was extremely difficult for her. In our first session, Karla explained that she trusted few people. I asked why. She told me it was very difficult for her to trust because she had been repeatedly disappointed. In her words, people used what they knew about her inappropriately. Consequently, she was very restrained in her trust of others. When I asked her what she feared, Karla replied, "I don't know.... I think feeling vulnerable." Does that sound familiar to you? Who wants to feel vulnerable? I don't know anyone who enjoys being vulnerable.

I have been practicing an exercise of welcoming and accepting my vulnerabilities. It is not an easy task. However, I have decided to adopt this practice as part of my personal growth because recent sociological studies show there is power in accepting and sharing our vulnerabilities because it requires a sense of self-confident and worthiness.

We don't want to be vulnerable because it has negative connotations. It puts us at a disadvantage because it can negatively impact our image. However, vulnerability can generate positive emotions such as love, sense of belonging, enjoyment, and empathy. Brene Brown, a professor and researcher at Houston Graduate Collage of Social Work, says certain cultures are in an empathy crisis. United Estates is a good example, because we don't allow people to be vulnerable and without vulnerability there is little empathy. We need to show our emotions, expose our failures, open ourselves up so others can connect with us empathetically. Otherwise, there is no real empathy. Creativity and innovation also arise from vulnerability. There cannot be creativity without vulnerability. Being creative entails being comfortable exposing ourselves publicly to failure and success.

Karla didn't know this. We have grown up believing that we cannot fail or show our weaknesses. Brené Brown discovered that people who have the courage to be imperfect, to have compassion for themselves, to connect with who they really are and accept their weaknesses, feel highly valued and appreciated by themselves and others. While people who do not accept or connect with their vulnerability usually feel they are unappreciated or not good enough. This is where I write; "I am proof of that."

From a very young age, my parents taught me I was special. What made me supposedly special was my extrasensory ability to see and perceive other sets of consciousness and situations that were not tangible to others. I grew up believing I had something few others had. I clung to that belief as a model of behavior. I unconsciously thought I could not fail and had to be an example for others to follow. I also believed I had to save others and, in some way, protect them. I did not realize until a few years ago that wanting to protect and help others was good provided I did not feel it was my responsibility or meant suffering and anguish for me, which was often the case.

This belief caused me high levels of stress and constant fear of loss due to violent that put the physical and emotional integrity of those who I was supposed to look after at risk, including myself. My survival mechanism remained activated, my demands for myself were very high and all of this happened because I believed I was special. My biggest lesson learned was that we are all special in some way, that we all have the same abilities regardless of whether we have developed them or not. To understand that it was OK to be vulnerable brought me peace and allowed me to be who I truly am. As I released myself from the responsibility of being the protector, I was freed from high levels of stress that caused my body to react with shock and anger when others were attacked or faced injustice. Now I can feel coherence, where before there was anger and defense.

New social studies are inviting us to accept vulnerability as an element which generates empathy and at the same time social strengthening where we recognize the vulnerability of others in our own vulnerabilities. I believe that at the end of the day, this allows us to be who we truly are and not what we think we should be. But we have learned to be competitive and to not show our weaknesses to survive. At present, we see how we gather as small tribes and seek to reaffirm what the tribal leader says, so we can retain support from the group. When people decide to disagree and suggest other possibilities by going against the leaders, they run the risk of being expelled from the group. It takes courage to overcome the fear of rejection when searching for new alternatives of life. This is why a new and authentic model of leadership requires transparency, to accept one's own vulnerability in front of others and show his or her true self. In this model of leadership, the tribe would never follow leaders for their physical strength or skills to overcome challenges, but because of their authenticity, ability to activate power in others, to help them see they have the same capabilities to achieve. In this model the leader is a guide, not a protector.

I asked Karla about her romantic relationships and how satisfying they were. She responded with an ironic smile that her relationships ended even before they started, as she knew in advance that the relationship would eventually end. Karla unconsciously chose relationships which from the beginning posed a cultural or ideological separation. Her partners end up moving to another country or, because of religious beliefs, didn't connect. When we explored what was good about this survival mechanism, we discovered that she was afraid of being abandoned. She had an unconscious program of not committing to anything, including not having children, so she would not go through the same pain of not being recognized by her father (first abandonment), the pain of an absent mother (second abandonment), and the loss of her mother at an early age (third abandonment).

Karla established relationships in which she knew what to expect. She knew they would end abruptly, and she was ready for it. Her mind created that mechanism to "protect" her from a greater unexpected pain. When I pointed out that every way she was losing and eventually she was abandoning herself, she began to see things differently. Karla has probably continued in an amygdala hijack due to her traumatic childhood. Since she was very young she was subjected to abrupt and imposed changes, like moving from one country to another, living with people who were not familiar, the abandonment of her mother, and the hostility of her family. What made these events even more traumatic was that whenever a change occurred, she was in danger of dying. She fell down a tree, almost drowned in a river, and fell off a horse. She never received the necessary support to recover from the traumatic stress of these events. Karla overcame all of them by herself.

What our minds do to protect us from what it considers an attack on our physical or emotional integrity is amazing. But what we really need is an adaptation mechanism. One of the goals I worked on with Karla was to regain sleep capacity. She just slept a few hours a day. She said her mind was continually active and she could not rest. During our second session, when I invited Karla to describe her feelings and not what she thought, she said she was not used to feeling. She occasionally did some extreme things like getting a tattoo or bungee jumping to remember what "feeling" was like. Karla had blocked her emotions because of the high and constant level of pain she had been exposed to.

Karla had reached such a stress point from all these traumatic events without the support and love of her parents that her way of surviving was anesthetizing her emotions. What Karla did not know is that it is impossible to anesthetize only negative emotions. Once you anesthetize pain, anger, anguish, or sadness, you also anesthesia positive emotions like love, enjoyment, and happiness because there is no way to feel selectively. When you become insensitive to some emotions you become insensitive to all.

Karla developed a rational personality with the need to

control everything, including her interactions with friends, the future of her romantic relationships, and even her sleep. Because she felt so threatened by her environment, her mind told her she should stay vigilant. Therefore, she suffered from insomnia. Even when she managed to sleep, she dreamt about being observed by herself, as a mechanism to feel that she continued monitoring herself in case something bad happened.

Karla is an example of how those painful first life experiences and feeling at risk activates our survival mechanism and conditions us. Fear of pain or emotional injury also forces us to take extreme measures, as if we were at risk of dying.

Here lies the drawback of having developed a shortcut in our brain. Although it allows the amygdala to receive some signals directly from our senses so it can react quickly to imminent danger, it also triggers a hormonal secretion that determines our behavior before those signs are recorded by the neocortex, our creative, analytical, and strategic side. Making decisions without consulting them with the frontal lobe and other analytical areas of the thinking brain, which causes us to lose control, say things we regret and cause us to stay in an amygdala hijack, is the reason we do extreme things with the intention of avoiding danger and pain.

However, rationalizing our decisions does not necessarily mean success and happiness. We build our reality from our interpretations and although we rationalize them, reason is another filter as well as our senses. The amygdala simply seems more sophisticated and experienced through evolution. But although more detailed and refined, it is another filter with its own challenges as the so-called narrative fallacy. This is the mind's mechanism that seeks to complete information and build the most plausible stories when it does not have all the elements to decide. It makes the last evaluation on what emotions and intuition have already decided.

## Beyond Emotions

There is a human error we must correct. This error took place at the beginning of our civilization when we decided that we should gather in tribes to survive. But grouping us was not the problem. The error came after. It was believing we had to compete between tribes and start attacking each other, marking territories, and creating frontiers. Feeling threatened by others, we began to create socially accepted emotions from that tribe conception. We created the need to belong, to be valued, to be important and accepted so we would not be expelled from the tribe and put in danger. The impact this has had on our current society is devastating. We take those primary emotions that were developed to survive in situations of risk and apply them to our families, co-workers, and any human who thinks differently or who belongs to a different group.

Fear, whose objective was to protect and care for our species, was turned into fear to live. Affection, whose objective was bonding and connection, we turned into a privilege for just a few. A special gift for our tribe that contributes to our lack of empathy. Sadness, whose objective was to help us reflect and connect with ourselves, we turned into manipulation towards others, to make sure that they care for us and that they do not abandon us. Anger aimed to defend an imminent attack. We turned it into a way of expressing our unmet needs. Happiness, whose objective was the enlivening and the battering of our existence, we turned into a place to come, linking it to having instead of being.

Because of this error, we all at some point feel that we are not good enough or sufficiently recognized, or sufficiently valued or loved, or sufficiently attractive or successful, or smart enough. The list is endless. This feeling of not being good enough and feeling that no matter what we do we will always lack something, comes from that first mistake. From believing that we are detached from each other and from forgetting that we are the same species. This mistake developed by the ego in our mind, telling us that we must compete to be better or more special so we can have value. It is part of the belief that we are not worth anything unless we do something to be worthy, because the strategies we established to gain that value were all externally oriented.

This belief shared by humanity, that are not worthy unless we do a series of things to get value, has led us to believe.

- We must take care of our image more than ourselves.
- The more we have the more we are worth.
- We must work hard so people can see we are good, because "good" is accepted.
- We must do many things to be recognized.
- We must compete to excel because if we do not, we can lose our place in the world.
- We should focus on doing, instead of being.

Believing that we have no value and wanting to look outside ourselves causes us to reach a dead end. You will never reach enough and will always seek more because you will not be satisfied, looking for value outside of yourself, looking for others to give you the value that only you can give yourself or, to be more accurate, that only you can recognize yourself because the value is already a fact.

The solution then is to abandon the ego strategy and commit yourself to acquire coherence, to BE instead of DO, to recognize worth in yourself, in your essence, to be who you are and to identify the value that others have from being who they are. This does not mean that doing things is unimportant, but you will do things for the right reason, inspired by your essence and your true passion and not by the need to take care of your image or to win a place or status in the world.

When we recognize there is no need to compete for a space or place in the world because this is everyone's place, when we understand that we belong to the same tribe called humanity and the need to defend ourselves from others is not real because there is no a real attack, and that every human being wants to be happy like we do and that there is no one who deserves more or less than someone else, we will achieve freedom. We will be able to activate the original intelligence because we would have reached self-love, which we use to project ourselves to the world.

I believe that we are in an era of consciousness, where we are rethinking these old scenarios and ways of knowing and understanding, where we need to learn the language of the heart, to develop a new intelligence, where we are looking for alignment between what we think, what we feel, and what we do, because incoherence is destroying us as individuals, and as humanity. We think one thing, we feel different. We end up doing something contradictory. We betray ourselves.

Finding coherence implies establishing connection points. We need to understand our self-protection, which are those negative emotion shooters and their origin, so we can re-signify them. I have my own definition of what we call the triggers. For me they mean unresolved needs. For example, if social justice is a subject that is a trigger for me and when I feel that justice is not being done, it generates anger. That feeling is an indication that there is an unresolved need. If I search within my sensitivity to that topic, I might find that I may have been a victim of social injustice in the past or perhaps someone I care for was a victim of that injustice and unconsciously I acquired the commitment to not allow more injustice. That is how it became my trigger, so that sensitive subject reminds me of a need for justice. So, if I want this issue to stop being sensitive to me and not trigger my anger, I must heal the sensitivity, which is possible by re-signifying the experience.

That is, if I recognize that perhaps anger is a memory of what happened before and I become aware that every time someone speaks about social justice and thinks differently that person is not trying to attack me or to be unfair to me or to someone I care for but it is a new, different situation and that the result does not have to be the same as I remember, I can then create another connection to the subject and the trigger will decrease or disappear on its own. Then I will have some other way to react without condemning that specific person because of something that someone did in the past. Social justice will continue to be a topic of interest, but it will not activate my anger because it is not a personal attack. It will become a more unlinked experience in the present or future.

Identifying our negative emotional activators is an essential part of awareness. Without that step, we cannot acquire coherence. Illustrating the example mentioned before, coherence would manifest when instead of believing that I am angry about a social injustice, I recognize that what I feel is a reminder of something that happened in the past. What I am going to feel is going to reflect a vision of the present without preconceptions, and I consciously choose to take care of it and heal that experience so it no longer triggers negative emotions.

To heal that past, I need to go through the following steps.

1. I recognize what happened. I identified the event or stressful moment I lived.
2. I understand and identify what conscious or unconscious decision or commitment I developed from what happened.

3. I accept what happened (I cannot change but I can change my interpretation of what happened).

4. I release the emotions and interpretations about what happened.

5. I incorporate it into my life in a positive way, re-signifying it (I take what is positive about that experience. What did I learn from it? Which skill did I develop? How did it help me?)

Thoughts and emotions are energy in different fields. From a biological point of view, thought is a scenario, an unrevealed possibility, while emotion is a physiological reaction already revealed. Emotions provoke thoughts just as thoughts end up becoming emotions when they are persistent. These two determine our stability or survival. Our reasoning and emotionality are interrelated. They depend on each other. We need a catalyzing agent that neutralizes these two aspects which seem to be going in different directions, building the most plausible stories from the reality we observe but unfortunately always confirming our preconceptions and connecting with that we already know, perpetuating our past, our same point of view or what is known as confirmation bias.

The key is to become aware and transcend the conditioning and preconceptions that we previously established. Not by trying to change what we feel and rejecting it, but understanding that feeling and cultivating new emotions so that the others vanish, which is a big difference. It is not the same to focus on changing something negative than to focus on acquiring something positive, because when you say you want to stop feeling sadness, you continue to focus on sadness, you keep thinking about how sad you feel. Thus, it attracts more situations which confirm that feeling, while if you focus on being happy and do things that make you happy, you will be creating new neural connections for happiness.

Mary Helen Immordino-Yang says: *"without emotion, all decisions and outcomes are equal—people can have no preferences, no interests, no motivation, no morality, and no sense of creativity, beauty, or purpose…emotions are, in essence, the rudder that steers thinking".*

If psychological research and spiritual currents claim that having positive emotions is beneficial to our mental, physical, and emotional health, why do we strive to maintain negative emotions and justify them with our mental narrative? We become addicted to negative emotions without knowing that we select them unconsciously. An antidote would be to keep an open and curious mind towards new things, to always explore the questions, "What if this was different? How would it be?" And from there create our motivators. In other words, we step aside and allow the universe to show us other outcomes of that same story.

# THE FOURTH BRAIN AND THE ORIGINAL INTELLIGENCE

We have a fourth brain that lies in the heart, where there is real emotion. I say real because I consider that the other emotions originated in the amygdala are instincts of survival and recorded memories that are activated or deactivated according to the unconscious triggers that we have created. Those emotions, which our ego has created, are incoherent with our current purpose of life, for we no longer seek to simply survive. Although these emotions were valuable then, today they go against our happiness when they generate conflict by making us believe that we should take comments or the actions of others as personal attacks. The original emotion is in coherence, because it is not something we experience but it is who we are—love.

Let's look at emotional intelligence to understand where the original intelligence comes from.

Emotional intelligence was first introduced in 1990 by psychiatrists like Stanley Greenspan. Scientists John D. Mayer and Peter Lovey developed the topic and defined it as a form of social intelligence that involves the ability to monitor and differentiate our thoughts and emotions to guide our actions. They investigated ways to measure this intelligence and determine its impact on everyday life. Later, the psychologist Daniel Goleman would take up these investigations and expand the definition of emotional intelligence into a set of competencies that would determine someone's level of emotionally intelligent.

These competencies have been described and widely disseminated as follow:

Self-awareness: The ability to recognize what is felt and what is thought at every instant, also the impact these have on oneself and others. The ability to recognize our preferences and guide our decision-making, with confidence in our own abilities.

Auto-regulation: The ability to handle emotions so that they do not interfere with our daily activities, as well as our ability to recover from emotional stress.

Motivation: The ability to pursue our goals and objectives by having initiative and being effective in moving forward despite the obstacles and frustrations of the process.

Empathy: Realizing what other people feel and see and cultivating interpersonal relationships with others.

Social skill: The ability to manage emotions in relationships, being assertive when interpreting in a proper manner situations and social relationships, encouraging positive and healthy relationships.

For Goleman, the functioning of the amygdala in its interaction with the neocortex is the neurological nourishment of emotional intelligence. He describes it as a set of layouts or abilities that allows us to take the reins of our emotional impulses, understand the deepest feelings in ourselves and others, manage our relationships in a harmonious way, and having the ability to speak with the right person, in the exact degree, at the right time, with the proper purpose and in the correct way.

Each of us have experienced that sensation when someone says or does something that we dislike and it touches a sensitive fiber within us. We feel it on our chest, our heart beat increases, and we experience a sudden hit in this part of our body, and we clench our jaw. This happens when we are energetically closing towards the other person or people that offended us. We are blocking the flow of energy wanting to disconnect from others and we lose internal coherence.

However, changing our natural reaction during conflict situations and being able to exhibit these emotional intelligence skills is not possible through just rationalization or thinking about it. In the best scenario, we can hide our negative emotions from others and be polite saying phrases such as "I understand where you are coming from," but most of the time we really don't. We strongly believe we're right and we just say we understand to fake "respect." We believe that we obtain control of our emotions because we do not verbalize them or allow our face or body to reveal them. Even if we hide these emotions from others, what we feel continues to grow as a block of energy in our body and in our hearts because what we feel when our weak spots get triggered continues its internal path. Through this emotional control, we can change our behaviors, but not what we feel when we are triggered.

My intent is to go beyond Goleman's approach so we can get closer to another form of intelligence that transcends cognition and emotions, where we do not learn to understand our impulses to control them, but we decode and transcend them, we transform them by our original state. Where we are not guided all the time by our survival instincts, neither the amygdala, nor the reasoning, but the transpersonal aspect of the heart, which is our state of original consciousness and the only true emotion—LOVE.

To understand the term transpersonal, we will term personality that set of protagonists existing in our mind, which constantly claim to be masters of our actions. One way to describe the interaction of these protagonists is to remember when we assume roles in the face of certain situations. We can be very tender when we see the person we love, become warriors when our territory has been threatened, and become melancholy when the one we love prefers someone else. These roles we assume are archetypes and personalities that we adopt to respond to similar situations. Then we identify with those roles, and we create our identities. We believe that we are those characters, the bad-tempered, the pessimist, the incredulous, the victim, the perpetrator, or the hero. But the characters appear and disappear according to the circumstances and the environment. When we talk about transpersonal, we talk about the recognition and awareness that we have created those characters in our story, but we are not those characters. We are the observers behind those characters.

The real self is beyond the characters and roles we believe us to be. When we transcend those characters and roles we believe to be, we find a new field of consciousness. We are in the world of possibilities. We let out our potential, contemplate elevated states of consciousness where we see no attack but someone asking for love, where we do not feel fear but feel peace within ourselves and with others, where we do not get angry because we refuse to give meanings and judgments and in its place we understand. This is the result of our original and transpersonal intelligence.

Not everything in life is solved by thinking about it. To develop our self-consciousness or self-awareness, we must stop thinking to develop our attention, sensorial, and extrasensory perception. Our physical senses in fact are just good for survival. Self-consciousness has little to do with the process of thinking. It has more to do with feeling and being. So, the phrase of Descartes "I think then I exist" where he declares that the only way to find the truth is by thinking, is far from being true for me. If we consider that our cognitive reasoning is tied to our emotions and interpretations of the reality we observe, thinking will not lead us to the universal truth, but to the truth that each one of us wants to believe. This is verified with the experiment of the three slots of quantum physics which I explain in my book, "Quantum Empathy: The Path To Create Happiness And Success." This experiment concluded that the matter and the reality that we observe responds to the expectations of the observer, and that ultimately our expectations change the results. Therefore, thinking just guarantees one thing—projecting what we want to see on the outside.

As an alternative, feeling and connecting with our interior world offers us the truth of who we are. We perceive the moment as it is without expectations, only what is there, and we accept what there is without judging or changing it. We put aside the ego. This does not mean to do nothing when facing a situation, but to do from another place that is not our characters or our instincts. We express ourselves from our essence and only then our self-projection changes. The easiest way to explain this is to think of the scenario of an earthquake or a natural catastrophe. In that precise moment we forget our characters, we forget our grudges, differences and the social, cultural, economic, and even moral distances. We help others without knowing them. Our unconditional love is awakened. It has nothing to do with survival because if we just cared about our own life, we would do nothing for others. But that is not how it is. We help others because at that critical time the life of that other is the most important thing. When we help others without receiving anything in return oxytocin is released in our bloodstream. We feel good helping others for the simple reason of helping, as if what we did for them we were doing for ourselves, which in fact is so.

This new original intelligence proposal, although it may sound unattractive to organizations because talking about love does seems more like a family or personal concern, represents one of the easiest ways to understand ourselves and others—a consistent way to transcend and evolve as a species regardless of the environment in which we find ourselves.

From my experience as a therapist, coach, and facilitator of emotional intelligence programs, I can attest that the problems employees face in organizations are intimately related to their traumatic experiences or embedded beliefs of the past, which is reflected in the work environment. These experiences and challenges are always rooted in the belief they are not good enough and they have to do extraordinary things or have more titles and more money. They must defend themselves from the one who takes away their value or that they have to prove that they know more, so they can be approved, recognized, respected and loved. For this reason, organizations become competitive spaces where people seek to excel at all costs, but basically what everyone wants is to be given love.

Thus, believing that it is inappropriate to talk about love at work is like asking a human body to stop growing fingernails. It like telling employees not to become aware and to try to solve their problems without knowing the causes. With this approach we will end up prescribing solutions that can remove the symptoms without eradicating the underlying problem. Then the symptom will be repeated even if the employee is relocated to another position or even if they change jobs and interact with other people. Our reality is internal and follows us wherever we go. The only way out is to change the way we perceive things so that the things we perceive change.

When we make decisions guided by anything but reasoning, we do not always use the instincts of survival. Sometimes we use our original intelligence, a compassionate impulse that responds to our true origin and respect as a species, which is reflected as a loving response to the other.

The original intelligence requires raising awareness, transcending the tendencies of our personality and acquiring a new framework of connections where no value is sought because I have it, where I do not seek love because I know that I am it, where I do not need to defend myself because I know it is impossible to be attacked unless I so interpret it, where I understand that every being in the world wants to be happy just like I do, and what people do or say is not expressed with any other intention.

# CHAPTER 4

# THE NEW PARADIGM

Let's identify this new Original Intelligence, its transpersonal aspect, and its structure.

From the standpoint of quantum physics, thoughts and emotions are energy and information in motion. They simply originated in different areas of our body.

If I ask you, what are you thinking right now? You would probably look in your mind. But if I ask you, what are you feeling now? You would look in your heart. Thoughts are stored in the brain, reproduced and amplified through the neural connections in our brain. The interesting thing is that the heart also has neurons and an organization very similar to the brain in our head. Canadian neurologist Dr. Andrew Amour discovered a sophisticated collection of neurons in the heart organized with a complex independent nervous system. This nervous system of the heart possesses about 40,000 neurons called sensory neurites, which communicate with the brain in the head.

This implies an intimate connection and communication between the brain and the heart. The idea that the brain controls what we feel is wrong. The heart is the only organ that has the property to send more information to the brain than it receives. About 400 times more, than the brain sends out to the rest of the body. Thanks to those elaborated circuits of the heart, it can make decisions and lead us to actions without consulting the brain.

The heart can learn, remember, and perceive. It has an independent memory apart from the mind memory. This was demonstrated during experiments at HeartMath Institute where people were hooked up to EKGs and other devices to measure their responses. Participants were shown pictures of frightening incidents, such as car crashes as well as pleasant pictures of puppies. Every participant showed the same neurological response. It was found that the heart responded by slowing down five seconds prior to the appearance of a highly stimulating picture. This stablish a path where is the hearth memory who sent the information to the brain of the head and then the head send the information to the gut to produce a response in the body. Which is different from muscle memory that it does not storage information on its own but in the brain. This is one of the main discoveries that marks a new paradigm in emotional intelligence.

There are four types of communication that start out from the heart and go to the brain. The first type is neurological communication which transmits nerve impulses. It can inhibit or activate certain parts of the brain according to the circumstances. The second type is the biochemical communication which uses hormones and neurotransmitters, with which the heart produces the hormone ANF, or atrial natriuretic factor, which ensures the general balance of the body, called homeostasis. The heart also inhibits the production of the stress hormone and releases the love hormone called oxytocin. The third type is biophysical communication through palpitations, through which the heart rhythms and its variations sends messages not only to the brain but to the whole body.

The fourth type of communication is energy communication. The heart has the most potent electromagnetic field of all organs of our body. It is 5,000 times more potent than the electromagnetic field of the brain, and it extends around the body between two to four meters, depending on each individual. Those around us can receive the energetic information contained in our heart. This tells us a lot about our interpersonal and social influence. Even if there is no spoken communication, the interaction exists at an energetic or quantum level as well as the non-local level. I will not dig into the non-locality because it is a large topic for another book.

This electromagnetic field changes according to our emotions. When we have negative or positive thoughts, emotions like anger, fear, and stress make this field lose coherence and order, while emotions like love, compassion, and joy keep the field in order and harmony. This is why Ima Sanchís, author of the book "The Master of the Heart," concludes that "the love of the heart is not an emotion, it is a state of intelligent consciousness." And this agrees with other perspectives and spiritual currents. The book "A Course of miracles" says that love is our natural condition. It is our origin and not something we just experience, but who we are. By connecting with the fourth brain, we connect with the wisdom that spiritual traditions have called "The true Wisdom," which comes from the heart.

If love is what we are, and it is our state of intelligent consciousness, then resentment should be eliminated from our lives because it goes against what we are. It is the antithesis of our intelligent consciousness. Resentment makes us clumsy, generates incoherence, disconnection, and puts us in survival mode. We then cannot create new scenarios but must persist on the same path, the one in which we are unconsciously condemning ourselves. Resentment makes us the cancer cells of society. We begin to work isolated from others and it generates complications with our family, social, and universal systems.

The heart influences more aspects of our life than we thought. It influences our perception of reality and our way of thinking. Our reactions are subject to the dialogue between mind and heart. The heart guides the mind. The brain is synchronized and follows the waves of the heart through the variations of the cardiac rhythm, leading to some interesting next questions. Does objectivity come from the heart or from reasoning? Is there objectivity or is coherence a better concept?

The heart brain is the key to getting out of the labyrinth of our unconscious. The heart activates in the head's brain new centers of perception of a completely independent and superior level that allows us to construe reality without leaning on past conditioning experiences or prefabricated emotions. It acts from a pure consciousness, clean of negative memories and conditionings of survival. This is how we can see reality from another point of view, without so many filters, and gradually this can create new circuits and neuronal associations that go beyond our personality, entering the scope of transpersonal. That is why I suggest coherence as the new and real objectivity.

This is not a science fiction book, although I know it seems like it. The latest scientific discoveries in neurology, cardiology, quantum, and non-local physics leads us to realities that had been imagined and personified in fiction films and books in the past, but today they are part of our world. Perhaps we should be more careful with what we imagine and think because we create our own reality.

Studies from "The Heart Math Institute" have scientifically demonstrated that when we activate the heart brain through rhythmical respiration or meditation, we create a state of coherence, where everything harmonizes in our body. This is measured by devices that calculate cardiac rhythm and neuronal activity in the brain. This is something I prove day to day with a device that reads the coherence of the heart called

EmWave2. I use it in my workshops and with it I measure the coherence of the participants while practicing a rhythmical respiration. This to demonstrate how a simple practice of mindful breathing can create coherence in the heart and brain. Through this device I can observe the effects of respiration on the heart rate, in the states of anxiety or stress and the ability to solve problems or think creatively.

We also activate that superior intelligence when we develop positive emotions. Not by the emotions themselves, but because those positive emotions are much closer to our original state. The closer we feel to gratitude and unconditional love the stronger the electromagnetic field and we develop more coherence. Not surprisingly, the biologist, genetic researcher, photographer and Buddhist monk Matthieu Ricard is seen by many as the happiest man in the world. Ricard meditates on compassion and love and says that the secret of happiness is becoming aware that we are not our emotions. This awareness makes those emotions gradually lose strength, and enjoyment then arises as a natural state of our being. In Qigon, a Chinese self-healing technique, 70 percent of our internal energy is increased by cultivating compassion, selfless help, and altruism, and the other 30 percent is increased through breathing. This makes sense if we consider that the heart increases its electromagnetism with altruistic emotions and love, creating coherence in the rest of our body. Rhythmic respiration generates coherence in the heart beat, which leads the brain of the head to acquire high levels of clarity, creativity, and decision-making capabilities.

This does not mean we have to become monks or saints twenty-four hours a day. My proposal is to adopt another more advanced and simple method of intelligence that requires less effort and control from our part, where it is not about monitoring our thoughts and emotions to control them. My proposal lies in acquiring consciousness transcending, the emotions, connecting ourselves with whom we truly are to go beyond our personality and recognizing our natural qualities of coherence, peace, wisdom, purpose of life, and love.

I have experienced going from feeling annoyed and frustrated by the attitudes of others to feeling love and acceptance for them. I achieved this by putting aside the characters I created of myself and others and opening a new mental canvas where I draw and paint freely without repeating someone else's work. Where every line I draw on that canvas I recognize as mine, even if I see it from the outside taking the faces of the people around me, I will always recognize them as my own because I am aware that there is no other way that they could have ended up there unless I drew them.

I find the book "A Course of Miracles" of great help to acquire coherence, although its name frightens many by its religious or magical connotation. I do not like religions, but this magnificent book does not really speak of how to work miracles but is dedicated to training our minds to correct mental errors, our emotions, and thoughts that have emerged from our interpretation of reality from our mind's perspective and the distorted directions of fear and ego—and that is what is called "miracle." The book says this is the only way to achieve internal coherence and know who we truly are. For me, it has been an extraordinary help.

# The Importance Of The Heart Brain In Our Health

The three venues of body communication are sensation, emotions, and sickness. As I mentioned before, we all have biological needs such as breathing, eating, having a safe place, relationships, etc. During unexpected circumstances, those needs may not be satisfied and when this occurs, it produces a biological impact or bio-choc. A bio-choc is the fortuitous encounter of an internal need with an external reality that is inadequate. Imagine that you need to feel supported under difficult circumstances. However, there is no one around to support you. This conflict creates a sensation in your body such as an empty stomach, back pain, shoulder tension, or a headache; that is the first communication attempt from our body to let us know that there is an unsatisfied need. If we do not pay attention to those sensations, to be aware of what our body is experiencing and why, the sensation will transform into an emotion such as abandonment, sadness, anger, or irritation. This is the second attempt of communication. When we ignore those emotions, suppress them, and decide to distract ourselves with something else, perhaps avoiding the feeling or denying what is happening for some period, the emotions transform into sickness, and this is the last attempt of communication from the body.

We have three significant ways of handling emotions: suppression, escape, and expression. The suppression is the most common road we take when we do not know what to do with the feelings we experience. We put emotions a side and try to keep functioning on our day-to-day life. However, the emotions that we put aside continue to grow and manifest on us later as irritability, muscle tension, insomnia, indigestion, allergies, etc.

The mind rationalizes everything to keep the emotions supposedly under control. To suppress emotions, the mind uses the denial and projection mechanisms. The denial appears when we have guilt or fear, we suppress what we feel and we deny its present within us. The projection is blaming external events and other people for what happens to us. In other words, the mind victimizes us. Suppressed feelings and emotions seek an outflow, so we look for excuses to justify what we feel and to not address the root of emotions. This mechanism in psychiatrist is called "displacement." We believe that certain situation makes us angry or sad, when in reality we are displacing anger to the situation as a way of not taking responsibility for the primary or true emotion that is within us and that is only stoked by the external events that we attract with our magnetism. Thus, the person who is afraid attracts experiences that cause fear. The person who is angry inside is surrounded by circumstances that make him/her angrier. We resist what we feel and that gives emotions more strength and power over us.

The escape mechanism for handling emotions is much utilized in today's days. People find all kinds of entertainment that become addictive. You escape your emotions by shopping, gaming, watching TV, eating, doing drugs, drinking alcohol, having sex.

The expression mechanism use to be my preferred choice until I understood the down sides of it. When we express negative feelings, we only let a portion of the inner pressure to go out. After that, we suppress the remainder of the emotion and put it out of our awareness. Verbalizing and venting what we feel could sound like a good idea to free ourselves from the feelings. However, the true is that expressing propagates that negative energy when I justify my feelings it damage relationships even more. Communicating is a positive approach only when there is no blame behind it. Taking responsibility of our emotions is the key to emotional maturity.

If we experience a stressful situation that is unexpected, emotions arise and the stress could create a bio-choc that brakes coherence and homeostasis in the body. We get sick because we stop listening to our body, our needs. We sacrifice for others, we do things because they are politically correct, but not because it is what we want to do or what we need to say. The first thing we do when we get sick is try to get rid of the symptom. Instead, the only thing we need to do is let go, is be conscious about our body and emotions. This does not mean not taking the medicine or not going to the doctor. It means going to the doctor or taking the medicine at the same time that I listen to what is the body telling me, and what is the connection between my symptom and my current life situation.

We must let go, stop resisting emotions, make ourselves aware of what our needs are, and allow emotions to be, flow, and manifest while we adopt an observer position. It is also important not to judge our emotions or feelings as good or bad, not wanting to change them or expressing them to others as if they were responsible for what we feel, because that would mean that we have identified with those emotions. It is the resistance and desire to control and change our emotions that feeds them even more. We simply observe how the energy of those emotions flow and manifests itself in our body as physical sensations. We understand their passage from a consciousness of unity. We observe them pass and by not rejecting them, that energy will continue its course and it will turn off by itself while we remain in coherence.

To maintain coherence, we must stop paying attention to the thoughts we have about the emotion we experience. These thoughts only reproduce each other. They reinforce ideas and judgments that end up making us believe that emotion is justified by external things that are foreign to us. We will begin to displace again on the outside, repressing the true cause. Then, our cells believe this information and end up manifesting in the body as a disease. We must have self-awareness, recognizing that it is our own projection and displacement. If we are experiencing a strong physical sensation, it is because there is an accumulated energy due to the unconscious suppression that we have made of some emotion.

From an energy point of view, we can also affirm that when the mind does not listen to the impulses and intuitions of the heart, sickness appear. The brain of the head is affected by magnetic fields, especially the magnetic field of the heart. In addition to that, when we alter the magnetic coherence of our heart with our negative thoughts or suppressing emotions, this creates internal disconnection. The heart sends information to the brain of the head, altering its magnetic field as well. This produces a physiological response in the body, changing the information of our cells. Through the awareness and acceptance of hidden or repressed emotions, we can have a better quality of life and wellbeing.

The principles of coherence lie in correcting the three errors I will explain in the next chapter.

CHAPTER 5

# THE THREE ERRORS TO CORRECT

When I speak about coherence, I refer to the ability to make what we think, feel, and do the same thing. In other words listening to your heart. That is why I say it is one of the greatest challenges for any human being. Generally, we think something, we feel something else, and we end up doing something completely different.

Humans are born in coherence. When we are born, if we feel like crying we cry, if we are hungry we are fed, if we feel sleepy we fall asleep, and if we want to touch something, we do it. It is an innate coherence. We do what we feel and we demand what we need, and if we do not receive it we weep and communicate our needs.

When we grow up that vanishes and most of the time those three aspects (what we think, feel, and do) are misaligned. They do not correspond to each other and are incoherent. This is due to three fundamental errors.

1. We believe that we are detached from others. When we are separated from our mother at birth, we develop this idea of separation that is limited to our physical body because we are energetically connected

and inseparable. However, this belief in separation generates a feeling of loneliness that is emphasized when we grow up and become self-sufficient. Consequently, we create the need to be accepted, admired, and recognized by others—starting with mom and dad and then socially. We start special relationships, we want to be special to others and that being "special" establishes hierarchies in such a way that being special for someone implies preference over others and that is how we cultivate the idea of being closer or bonding to someone.

Then we unconsciously judge what we feel, think, and do. We do not allow ourselves to feel or think differently from what others expect from us. We are afraid to be ourselves and end up doing what others assume we should do or what we believe is our duty to do. If at some point we decide to do what we really want to do, we feel guilty or do not forgive ourselves for doing so. Correcting this error implies recognizing that there is no such separation and that we are a constant reflection of others just as others are a constant reflection of ourselves. Even what bothers us so much about others implies there is a part of myself that bothers me and that in some aspect of my life I behave in a similar way.

It is healthy to express ourselves as we are, surrendering that need to be accepted by what is outside, and this begins by accepting and loving ourselves with our strengths and weaknesses. When we achieve this, self-acceptance is responsible for generating the acceptance of others as a natural effect, inherent to the connection that I have with the whole. I need to see the other one, son or daughter, friend, husband, wife, or boss as my teacher from whom I need to learn. And the most beautiful thing is that he or she is teaching me something about myself that I could not otherwise see.

2. We believe in punishment. We are conditioned by experiences of the past (this includes not only our first experiences but our prenatal experiences and the experiences of our ancestors because we inherited them). Therefore, we act reactively, defending ourselves from what we believe is an attack or repetition of a previous fact. We justify our attacks on others by arguing our defense. But the truth is we are never mad about that specific reason. We get angry because we interpret what happens to us from a similar experience of the past and that unmet need calls for revenge. Correcting this error implies recognizing that the attack is an illusion. If I see an attack from someone towards me, it is my own projection or an attack that I am doing to myself through the other. We must let go of the need to defend ourselves and understand that in my helplessness is my power. When I say helplessness, I mean our ability to remain intact, focused, in coherence, understanding that no one can really attack me unless I decide to attack myself by interpreting the external facts as real attacks.

From a spiritual point of view, we can say that we forget who we are and why we were born, and we end up accusing others of what we agreed they would do to us when we arrived here. Since before birth, we choose our life and experiences to live. We choose the people who will join us on this trip and the challenges to learn to remember who we are. But we forget. Correcting this error implies accepting that the other is my teacher, teaching me the lessons that we agreed on before, and being thankful for the experiences and lessons which have allowed us to achieve through our interaction with them. I should add that the greatest awakening of consciousness usually comes from our most traumatic and painful experiences. Emotional and physical pain have an exceptional value in our evolutionary process because otherwise we would not see what we need to see, nor would we have paid attention to that aspect of our life if it were not for that painful experience. This does not mean that we only learn through pain. We can learn from another level of consciousness if we are more awake.

Painful experiences seem to be the path we choose the most. Many say, if someone shoots me with a gun, that's a real attack. But if that happens, the person who shoots would not be shooting you but themselves, or to what you represent in that person's mind. In reality, it is not an attack on you. On the other hand, when you receive the shot you are projecting an attack on yourself and this person, your teacher, would be reflecting your own anger and aggressiveness or the aggressiveness of your family story. Forgiveness is essential to correct this error and it is much more rational than to hate or resent because forgiving frees us from the past. It allows us to live the present, liberates us from the punishment we have imposed on ourselves thinking that we have imposed it on others. But by continuing to resent what happened, we are perpetuating the facts and carrying that weight to the present. That is irrational because we end up doing more damage by sustaining it for years than the same event that happened in a day or a few hours in the past. We believe that we are punishing the other when we are actually punishing ourselves.

3. We believe in control: Believing that we have control of our life is an illusion. We believe we control our lives and what happens by doing things, working, convincing others of our point of view, judging whether what we do is right or wrong, telling others what to do and how to do it. We always believe we are right and we go through life believing that what we do is the best. We believe that as more things happen the way we want them to happen the more control we have. The illusion of control lies in its source and purpose. Our source of control is rooted in the first two errors. The idea of separation and the idea of justice or punishment, which we have manufactured from the prejudices and beliefs of what we must become or do to fit into society, to be recognized and accepted and not expelled from the tribe. If this is the source of our control, we understand that we are not controlling anything. Rather we are being controlled by our past experiences, our fears and prejudgments, which condition our decisions and actions.

The purpose of control is to feel safe and this makes control unsustainable. When we face the first unforeseen situation, or it is out of our controlled plan, we feel insecure, frightened, frustrated, and powerless. We refuse to accept what happened. We reject it and go against the current to regain control. We believe we know what we need, that we will achieve it only in our plan, and that the only answers or courses of action are those we conceive. We ignore a whole arsenal of causes and circumstances that are acting behind the scenes, causing unexpected events in our lives that are in complete coherence with what is happening inside us because those things are responding to our real needs. There is a higher order that organizes these events and helps us to generate these opportunities for our own growth and awareness. I call this the homeostasis of the universe.

Correcting this error implies letting go and giving up the need to control. It implies accepting and welcoming with love what happens to us as if it were our special guest. We replace control by a desire to flow, to be guided by uncertainty with humbleness. Recognizing that we do not have all the answers and that there are other better and safer ways for our integral development as human beings—acquiring the attitude of visitors (that I will explain later). We do our part and let the universe do the rest. This does not mean that we do not have goals. It implies having goals but welcoming whatever happens to us as an opportunity to grow and as something we need to see to recognize, learn, transcend and finally integrate it into our life as a lesson learned. This way we will get faster and safer to our goals and expand our ability to project ourselves in the world, manifesting consciously.

CHAPTER 6

# How To Make Our Transformation Sustainable

What makes our behaviors, emotions, and reactions difficult to change is not the lack of skills, will, or effort. The difficulty of making change sustainable is that we focus our efforts on the wrong place and we can't let go.

There are different neurological levels that intervene in the process of human change. According to the model of neurological levels for change and learning of Robert Dilts, there are six dimensions present in each human experience, hierarchically organized in such a way that each level organizes and directs the interactions in the lower level. We organize our thoughts and perceptions about the world and the meanings we assign them and the way we respond to them at different levels in the following way.

**Environment**: It is the temporal and spatial environment where a certain activity takes place and the characters involved in that activity. Neurologically, the perception of the environment is determined by how we capture the environmental information with each of our senses and the peripheral nervous system that receives the information and transmits it to the brain of the head so that it generates adaptive responses to the environment.

Changes at this level serve to accompany and reinforce changes previously made to other higher levels but do not generate a great effect by themselves. For example, I can change where I work, but I continue having the same type-controlling boss because the challenge is not on the environment, the challenge is probably on my belief system.

**Behaviors**: These refer to what we do concretely, the attitudes and actions that we take at a given moment. This level also includes thoughts that are not tangible or verifiable by other people. Thoughts that activate the same neuronal connections as if we perform the action. For example, neurologically thinking "I will end this relationship" is the same as ending it in action because it activates the same neuronal connections. I can try to change my lack of self-esteem behavior, but if I do not modify the beliefs that supports that behavior, change will not be permanent. I will always get back to what I believe is true. Neurologically, this level works with the motor system that directs physical actions and conscious movements.

Changes at this level can transform our behaviors at least for certain periods of time under certain circumstances, and in turn has an effect at the level of the environment that surrounds it.

**Capabilities**: These refer to how we do things, the skills we have developed to carry out behaviors or attitudes. They include all the strategies we have designed to achieve what we want, as well as our mental maps of reality and the recognition of the resources we must achieve it. For example, we can develop great communication skills to make sure we can express our rights because it give us a sense of peace.

Neurologically this level involves the development of the cognitive capacities of the cortical system with semi-conscious actions that manifest as groups of behaviors and actions that respond to a certain plan and mental map of reality.

Changes at this level can lead us to acquire new skills to learn new ways of doing things or face situations, and it influences the two lower levels, changing the behaviors and in turn the environment in which they occur.

**Beliefs and Values**: This level is one of the most complex. It involves all our personal ideas and important convictions. At this level, we harbor all that we have learned throughout our lives, about how things should be, what we value, how we should live life, and what is correct. Reaching a value can motivate us to action and develop capacities to achieve them. To ask why we do something leads us to identify our beliefs and identify the values we are seeking.

To improve our beliefs, we must be aware of them and clear

about where they come from and how they were developed. Only then will we understand why things happen to us daily because we will understand the belief behind those events.

Beliefs and values are unconscious responses that are part of the autonomous system. Neurologically, beliefs are related to the limbic system that manages emotions and long-term memory.

Changes at this level have a great impact on our lives. By transforming our beliefs, we can transform most of our life experiences because all behavior or attitudes have a belief and value that sustain them. For example, if I believe love is sacrificing, all my relationships will have some of that sacrifice, but if I transform my beliefs about love, understanding where this idea of sacrificing came from, I can transform my relationships.

**Identity**: This level is where all the aspects of who we believe to be are consolidated, everything we identify with, and the labels that we have assumed as our own. For example, you can consider yourself as perfectionist, hard-worker or terrible.

Our perception of our identity is related to the immune system, the endocrine system, and other functions related to the sustaining of life as our identity begins to give us a place in the world.

The changes at this level have an impact on all the lower ones and can reorganize aspects of our personality. Because we no longer identify with a certain role, it loses meaning for us and changes our beliefs, behaviors, and attitudes, thus impacting our environment.

There are behaviors that are confused with identity. We identify with what we do and believe those behaviors are who we are, like when we act rebellious in our adolescence and believe we are rebels without cause, when we are actually facing temporary reactions to a specific moment. That is why in this level of experience we find our shadow (those aspects not transcended of our personality, and which we reject of ourselves) and our ego (that character that thinks for us, the voice in our head).

**System**: At this level we find everything that goes beyond identity are the systems to which we are a part and that transcend our individuality, as well as the major systems to which other systems belong, such as the family belonging to society. This belonging in turn belongs to a country, the country to the planet, the planet to the universe, and the universe to the galaxy.

At this level we find the reasons why we are here and the real vision of our existence. This level is also called spiritual because it is where we find that which exists above ourselves. This level is related to everyone's complete nervous system, which is related to other nervous systems to form a kind of collective nervous system that in other traditions and currents is called "collective unconscious," "spirit or group mind." The transformation that we make in each of these levels will transmit that change downwards, generating changes in the lower levels. The lower levels will have a weak effect in the higher levels because they are motivated and depend on the superior levels.

When a conflict manifests itself at any of these levels, all other levels are involved. However, the circumstances will determine the level at which we mobilize. For example, when we become independent adults and get our own space and a job, we are especially focused on developing the CAPABILITIES and skills that allow us to adapt to the job and independence. We pay attention to the ENVIRONMENT taking care of the people with whom we must interact as well as the way in which we must behave, and our CONDUCT in this new stage of our life. On the other hand, in certain moments of our life we begin to wonder if the place where we work satisfies us or if we believe that we deserve something different or better based on our IDENTITY and our BELIEFS. There are also times when we ask ourselves if what we do has a meaning beyond the personal, if we are making any difference in the world and this is manifested in the SPIRITUAL / SYSTEM level.

Now that we know the different levels, we can see that the changes in higher levels have greater permanence and influence on our lives, not only because higher levels work at more complex neurological stages, but also because higher levels are related to more internal aspects of our being. It is part of our inner nature and not of what happens around us. This is consistent with what I have pointed out earlier about how our outer world is always the reflection of our inner world.

Therefore, when we speak of a true transformation, our efforts must be focused on working our higher levels of experience, such as our life purpose, identity, beliefs and values to achieve a sustainable and effective transformation in all other levels of interaction and experience.

Starting from this frame of reference, the original intelligence would become part of the SYSTEM or SPIRITUAL level, where a new transpersonal awareness and approach to life will lead us to transform all other levels of our experience.

# CHAPTER 7

# THE ORIGINAL INTELLIGENCE MODEL

Below I will explain the components of the original intelligence model and how we can activate each one of them.

## Self-awareness

Being physically awake does not mean that we are registering the here and now using all our senses. The automatic activity of our brain records all these things of the present consciously or unconsciously, and then interprets them with or without our help. It makes us believe stories about what it believes is happening, but as I mentioned at the beginning of the book, the brain is designed to find and activate mental maps and complete the lack of information with the most plausible and well-known stories we remember from our previous experiences.

Self-awareness is the ability to live aware of our actions,

feelings and perceptions of our own experiences and those of others, to understand our emotions, thoughts and states of being. Self-awareness is activated by paying attention, living in the here and now. Paying attention to what we perceive with our senses in the present as we are experiencing them. All the bodily sensations are important and they communicate something to us, but when we don't pay attention to those sensations and what we live and observe in the present because we are distracted thinking about the past or the future, what happens is that the brain automatically takes control and interprets those past experiences, integrating them as they best fit into an old thought or habit.

Another way to activate self-consciousness is by adopting what I call 'the visitor attitude.' When we visit a new place, we usually have an attitude of respect for the place we visit because we have never been there. We know that it is remote to us, we do not know how to move around, what are the codes of conduct and therefore we let the people who live there guide us. We go around with an attitude of gracefulness not to break into the dynamics and synergy of the place. We ask what to do, we move with curiosity, we do not seek to change things, but we accept them for their beauty and, because they characterize the place, we seek to understand rather than impose. The same is true when we take a new job in a company. We acquire the attitude of the visitor, the new one. Then we walk with respect, we ask more questions, and talk less. Everything is new and we want to make good connections, establish good relationships, so we do not begin by imposing our ideas or believing that we know how things should be. From our perspective of outsiders and visitors we listen and let ourselves be guided. We ask and give our opinion respectfully and without the desire to convince anyone, but with the spirit of contributing. The visitor attitude helps us be humble, to respect each other and to preserve our original goal, which is to help and contribute in the world with our gifts and talents, but with humbleness and an attitude of service.

When we lose the visitor attitude, our perspective and approach to things, people, and situations change and we begin to lose ourselves in the ambition of power and the desire for control. At work, we want to climb, we start competing for a spot, we no longer share and we suffer. In interpersonal relationships we acquire the desire for control, we want the other to change and be as we expect him or her to be, we stop feeling arouse for new things, the desire to give the best of oneself, and the habit attached to the illusion of 'always' makes us behave as if that person we love was to be here all our lives. We stop surprising and feeling surprised and end up forgetting the main objective when it all started, when we were visitors.

To adopt the visitor attitude does not mean to renounce establishing roots. On the contrary, the roots are strengthened in our interior. We root from our interior and in our coherence, and thus we feel at home wherever we go.

Our attention should be focused on activating the original intelligence and not on operating it, because when activated it works by itself. If I am coherent and I keep active my connection with my inner-self and my original state of love, I do not need to create action plans or responses for the difficult situations of life because my actions and words will naturally correspond to my state of coherence. Therefore we have to focus on maintaining our coherence and inner connection, because the original intelligence is in charge of the rest and will manage it naturally.

For example, if I have a work meeting with a colleague with whom I have a lot of friction, instead of preparing a plan and saying "I am going to stay calm, I will not say anything, I will let him talk, I will keep quiet and control myself not to explode," I decide to focus on keeping myself in coherence, in love, keeping my breathe and observing myself curiously, exploring my bodily reactions during the interaction and my approach to that person will always be, "I am interacting with a part of myself that I want to learn from, and therefore I respect and value him/ her." What I do from there on I do not need to control or plan because it will be fine if I stay in coherence.

## Self-projection

Self-projection is the natural and automatic process that happens to every human through which we project our interior to the exterior. This projection is not limited to things or situations, but involves everything we experience on the outside, including relationships, interactions, people, work, financial situations, and health.

When we realize that we are more in touch with our surroundings and with others than we think, we understand that punishment does not make sense, that attacking the other goes against myself and that resenting what others do to me is as similar as looking in the mirror and getting angry with the mirror for standing in front of us to show our own image which we reject seeing. When we give up the desire to change others, to control others, "Our mirrors" to show only what we want to see about ourselves and not to reveal our shadows, we flow, grow, evolve, and stop suffering. Most of our suffering is not caused by what happens to us, but by what we think about what happens to us, by the meaning we give to what happens to us and not by the situation itself. For example, if someone lies to me and I discover the lie, what hurts me is not the lie but the fact of being betrayed, and the meaning I give to being betrayed, not by the situation alone. I could understand that the person who lied to me hid information because he or she was afraid to tell the truth and then I ask myself where in my life I am lying to myself and what is my fear of the lack of honesty towards myself. The lie remains undesirable, but instead of judging the other and condemning him or her for lying to me, I try to understand and establish new agreements and I thank that person mentally for showing me that aspect of myself that I had not been able to see.

## Empathy as part of self-projection

Empathy is part of self-projection and appears when what I project is a side of myself with which I identify. We feel inclined to help, support, and understand those who are like us.

Who does not want to look good and have a healthy and attractive body? Our physical body is what the world sees, it is the obvious. There are not many mechanisms to hide our defects and, if we manage to hide them, at the end of the day when we look in the mirror we know what our reality is. The same goes for our emotions, although sometimes we try to hide what we really feel so people cannot perceive or recognize those emotions. At the end of the day, our emotions are the same and in some cases their intensity increases because we resist them. The emotions remain there even if we try to hide them, ignore them, or stop paying attention to them.

As humans, we have a biological instinct to hide our imperfections and vulnerability. We are conditioned to show strength and hide our weaknesses, to pretend that we have power or that nothing affects us so we are not an easy prey. However, studies of sociology indicate that vulnerability is one of the main generators of empathy among humans. For example, when we see someone in distress or danger after a natural catastrophe, we instinctively try to help because we feel empathy.

From this new model of intelligence, when we have interpersonal problems, recognizing the vulnerability of the other helps us to understand him or her and ourselves in relation to the other. In the end, we understand that the vulnerability of the other is my own reflected vulnerability and that we have more things in common than we think with those we refuse to work with or relate to. On many occasions the rejection of the other is a way of rejecting our shadows through them, the non-transcended aspects of our personality.

When I was about 17 years old and I decided to tell my father personally how much I had suffered because of his absence, his abandonment and the things he told me the few times we saw each other. He lived in another city, about four hours by car. I took advantage of a family trip to that city to call him and tell him that I wanted to talk to him. I had gained strength and courage to tell him a few truths about his behavior and lack of care for me. I asked him to meet me in a nearby restaurant. When I arrived, he was a bit surprised and intrigued about what I had to say. I went straight to the point and talked to him about how abandoned I felt, how much I needed him during my childhood, and how angry I was to see that the few times we saw each other he always had a tragic story to tell or something negative to warn me about, filling me with fear and stress at a young age. As he always claimed he was waiting to have some money, I told him that I never needed his money because thank God my mother gave me everything. What I needed was his affection and support as a father.

After having my catharsis and venting the things I never told him, my father started crying. He could not stop. The sadness in his eyes frightened me and I was touched by his tears. Crying, he told me that I was right and he was wrong. He was probably doing what he had learned from his parents, because he also had been abandoned by my grandfather. He also told me that by thinking about being able to offer me some economic support, he never came back because work was going badly. When I heard his story and saw his tears, I realized that his pain was mine. But even more importantly, I felt empathy for him when he showed me his vulnerability. I had gone there to tell him how bad I felt and I had met someone more frightened and hurt than me. At that time, the vulnerability connected us on the level of the heart. Since then, our relationship changed positively. There was nothing to hide because everything was said.

Ironically, sometimes our strengths end up being our weaknesses. We develop strengths from the challenges we face in life. When we suffer as children from scarcity of money, we have the natural tendency to want to overcome that situation in the future and invest a large amount of our life trying to solve that. We work to defeat it and to ensure that it does not happen again. The challenge can be conquered, and the person gains a sufficient economical capital to live comfortably. However, by wanting to ensure that the challenge does not come back into our lives, something unexpected happens. It becomes a fear and that fear is our weakness. So, we gain money, but we develop distress about losing it. We believe that just as one day we did not have money, it may be gone again. This fear becomes your vulnerability even if you have achieved the goal, even if you have overcome the challenge at the material, mental, and emotional level, you think of scarcity and this creates an internal incoherence and unbalances you.

Transcending this implies letting go of the past and returning to our origins where we only take care of the present.

To understand our self-projection, when the conflict appears we must ask ourselves: What am I projecting? What do I need to see? And when something disturbs us a lot, ask: In which aspects of my life do I have the same behavior and I judge myself for it? When we are sick, we should ask ourselves: What is the role of the organ that has gotten sick and in which part of my life am I not fulfilling that function? Our life is a projection of our inner world, so we must care and cultivate our interior first and foremost. There is nothing on the outside that we see that does not exist within us. We only see what we want to see.

When we take responsibility for what happens to us, when we renounce judgement of what happens to us in life, the good or bad actions of others without wanting to control them, we become more coherent. We free ourselves from a heavy burden. We let the universe do its work, which it does anyway, but by stepping aside we allow things to flow more easily and quickly, to follow their natural course. This way we are happier and we acquire inner peace.

Through awareness, and the development of attention, taking the position of witnesses, visitors, observing our thoughts and emotions without judging, removing the power we have awarded them, questioning ourselves about which our real motivators are before taking action or a decision, and understanding that emotions do not determine what we are, but are an experience that is developing talents in us, we can achieve inner peace and consequently reflect it on our external reality. We must learn to trust in the heart's intuition and recognize that the true origin of our emotional reactions, triggers or unconscious motivators are not set in what happens in the outside. Instead, those emotional reactions are originated within us by those unmet needs that continue to hurt today and those deep-rooted beliefs that we need to transcend.

Self-projection is activated positively by cultivating the qualities of the heart, which include our original intelligence, being open towards our neighbor, listening and speaking from the heart, patience, cooperation, acceptance of the differences, stop believing and abandoning the ego strategy of looking for value outside of ourselves, recognizing our intrinsic value and that of others, without competing for a place in the world because I already have one, and understanding that competing with others is the same as competing with myself.

If we are positioned in our center of origin from which we see everyone as an extension of oneself, where there is no separation between the other and myself, and therefore I love and respect everyone equally, I can find inner peace and coherence. The triggers stop being activated because they have already lost sense. For example, if I previously resented the arrogance of someone, I will not bother because I understand that there is a part of my life in which I am being arrogant. I will laugh that life is showing me that through the other because I have not wanted to see it in me. I recognize it. I learn to be humbler in that fragment of my life, and that is how I integrate and release the trigger.

Coherence, in conjunction with self-projection, is achieved by living from the heart brain. It is to be free from the belief of separation and the three primary errors or mechanisms: fear, desire and craving for dominance or control. Mechanisms that are deeply anchored in every human because they have been our way to survive for millions of years. However, it is possible to transcend these conditions, to adapt to the world today where the goal is not to survive but to transcend.

## Inspiration

We need a new model of motivation. That's why I use the word inspiration instead of motivation, because motivation is linked to external things and situations while inspiration refers to inner reasons, deep in us, which do not disappear when something on the outside changes. The things that surprise and motivate us at some point in our lives gradually become unsatisfactory because our desire is set on getting superficial things—something better, bigger, higher position, higher income, more material goods, and more knowledge. If this momentarily drives us to grow, to continue forward and to improve, without coherence it becomes a lack of appreciation for what we have, emptiness and discouragement because when we get what we want it does not generate the satisfaction we expected. We end up complaining about our present and yearning for a different future. This is the chronic dissatisfaction of our time and lies greatly in internal incoherence, by not taking time to determine and connect with our life purpose, by not listening to that inner call telling us to do something transcendental for the people in general where we can express our essence, our unique talent and who we truly are. We are lost in the incoherence of doing because we do not have anything better to do. We're just filling up space. We do not know what we want to do. We think green, we feel white, and we end up doing blue.

How do we satisfy this animal of the false motivation that we have created? If we feed it every time it is starving, it will get used to it and it will want to eat more and more. If we submit it to periods of abstinence, hunger will create resentment and when we get a new achievement, we will not find satisfaction in it. We will look down on it. It seems that the only way out is to find coherence where what you need you get, what you have is valued, what is valued is pursued, what is pursued is accomplished and when we find something new, we welcome it not as something better than what we had, but as a complement to what we have. In other words, it is not acquired but is integrated.

The inspiration in this model of original intelligence refers to the will to connect with our purpose of life and to sustain an effort and interest to realize it and to manifest that purpose in our daily actions. This purpose of life transcends the personal interest and seeks to improve the world in which we live, not only for us but for all people. This does not imply sacrifice, on the contrary, the inspiration leads us to be happy doing what we like while helping others.

Daniel H. Pink, in his book "Drive," explains the three aspects that motivate human beings: autonomy, mastery and purpose. These three aspects are part of this model of inspiration, although raised from a more personal point of view, where I am free and autonomous to project myself in life as I want, in which I grow and develop talents from the challenges I face in life. I obtain authority and mastery of my talents as I express them and I carry out my purpose of life.

Inspiration in this new model of intelligence is our ability to connect with a transpersonal impulse, with those reasons that go beyond the individual and what is fleeting in our personality, reasons that move us and drive us forward permanently. This inspiration is not just about having a life plan, which is an important fragment because we need to establish a goal to achieve so we can acknowledge the direction we are going and why we are working for it. Although this inspiration also implies identifying the purpose behind each experience and recognizing that there is a purpose that inspires us to continue with the conviction, there will be personal growth from every experience, even those that we do not like. Thus, instead of resisting challenges and difficulties, we will accept them boldly. We know that behind these challenges there is an important learning process that has been specially designed for growth, not only personally but also as a group, family, and society.

## Contribution

By contribution, I mean the capacity to contribute in the world from our innate talents. The ability to connect with our purpose in life. This aspect of the original intelligence implies that we identify what our innate talents are, something that some call a divine or universal gift. This is determined by what we do well and without difficulty. It is what characterizes us and makes us unique in our contribution to the world. It is a talent that is given in a natural way and in which we find enjoyment or satisfaction, and it is sometimes not connected with our profession but with an ability to do or transmit something to others by providing a service that is not often requested by them. For example, we show empathy and understanding towards others so that we frequently find ourselves listening to their stories. To have the ability to guide others and lead so we can often meet with people who follow us or ask us for our advice to do something. It can also be an ability to help heal others physically or emotionally even if we are not doctors, or we can simply be providers of entertainment and fun times for others and we are just here to bring joy to those around us. Whatever our gift, we must identify it to express it with determination and purpose.

This intelligence impels us to seek to contribute from any place and from any role that we fulfill either in our work, in our homes or in our society.

## Coherence

Coherence is our original and transpersonal state of our being that expresses an intelligence to maintain our wellbeing. Coherence is the expression of the natural and balanced rhythm of the heart. When we develop the unity consciousness we remain in coherence, and the unity consciousness is acquired by practicing the four skills of the original Intelligence model: Self-awareness, self-projection, inspiration, and contribution.

The magnetic field of our hearts influences other magnetic fields, not only the magnetic field of other people, but also the magnetic field of the earth. Gregg Braden in its book Fractal Mind explains: *"Although we do not know many things about consciousness, there is one thing we know for sure: that it is composed of energy, and that magnetism is in that energy. A growing body of research suggests that terrestrial magnetic fields play an important role in connecting each other, as well as the planet."*

*"In September 2001, two geostationary metrological satellites (GOESs) orbiting the Earth detected an increase in global magnetism that forever changed the way scientists viewed our world and ourselves. The Goes-8 and the Goes-10, in the readings that transmit every 30 minutes, showed significant increases in the strength of the terrestrial magnetic fields.171 The Goes-8 detected, at 40,000 kilometers on the equator, an increase that reached almost 50 units more than usual 15 minutes after the first plane*

*crashed into the Twin Towers, and about fifteen minutes before the second impact."*

It is our responsibility to keep ourselves in coherence. Every emotion, every thought is impacting our magnetic fields, and the collection of our magnetic fields affect our surroundings. We are all one.

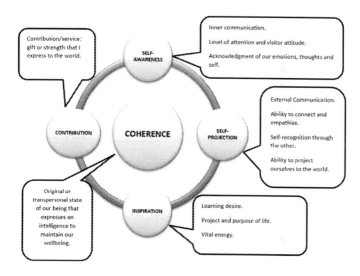

*Original Intelligence Model ©*

# CHAPTER 8

# Practices To Develop Original Intelligence

## Practice 1. Breathing and meditation

Learning to breathe is imperative to activate the original intelligence. When we focus on our breathing and develop a constant rhythm, we are connected to the present. For example, inhaling while mentally counting up to five, and exhaling while mentally counting up to five, and repeating this for 10 to 15 minutes while we focus our attention on the area of the heart helps generates coherence in the heart and cardiac rhythm, communicating to the brain of the head mental opening, activating creativity, and decision-making power.

Focusing your attention on the area of the heart while breathing rhythmically through the heart (using your imagination) and recreating feelings of compassion, love, fraternity and equanimity develops internal coherence and activates the brain of the heart.

Meditate focusing your attention on the present with each and every one of your senses without judging anything as good or bad, right or wrong, just appreciating and observing what is there such as thoughts or feelings, without rejecting or grasping. This practice provides openness and internal coherence. It takes us back to a zero state where everything starts again without a past or a future and the possibilities toward everything increases. You have to take care of your vibratory environment, collaborate with others, and altruistically help others to be happy. It is time to enjoy the little things of life in the present. All of this develops self-consciousness.

## Practice 2. Cultivate silence

We must cultivate silence, explore our interior in periods of solitude, connect with nature, contemplate how our thoughts pass by as clouds that we let go until we find spaces between thoughts. This is where we will find silence. Our internal dialogue is intense. We have about sixty thousand thoughts a day and most of them are negative. It is a wasteful dynamic in which we keep fragments of the previous day and we create others while anticipating future ideas. Cultivating silence helps us to calm this chaotic dialogue and save energy. However, our first mistake is to believe that to silence thoughts you have to stop thinking and leave your mind blank (free of thoughts). What this actually does is increase our thoughts and create stress and frustration. To achieve internal silence, you must begin by practicing mindfulness. That is to say, we do not speak physically and while focusing our attention on the present, emphasizing our breathing and the feeling within us. Mindfulness also requires focusing on our senses and sensations like sounds, smells, temperature. We can focus with eyes wide open on an object and perceive it entirely, discovering new characteristics or aspects that we did not see before, something we achieved only through observation or contemplation. Another way can also be focusing on an activity exclusively, without distractions and setting our full attention to every aspect of that activity and how we feel and experience it with our senses. This will cause the mind to automatically mute the other thoughts because it is exclusively focused on the sound, the process of breathing, a specific activity or an object to which we devote our full attention.

To reach deeper levels of consciousness and silence, practice transcendental meditation or any kind of meditation that focuses on cultivating inner silence. When you reach that silence, ask yourself:

1. Who am I?
2. What do I want?
3. What is my purpose in life?
4. What am I thankful for?

Ask the questions without preconceptions or looking for an immediate answer. Introduce the questions in the silence of your inner self and leave them there for your conscious mind to respond in its own time and using ways you cannot imagine. This practice develops self-awareness and inspiration and it works at the identity and system level.

## Practice 3. Take the visitor attitude

Constantly act as a visitor. Practicing the attitude of visitor is a choice that we can take daily in any area of our life. Ask more than what you say and do it with curiosity and an open mind to learn. Cultivate curiosity towards others and their motivations. Do not seek to change things to make them look more like what you are used to or how you think they should be. Understand them and learn from that new way of doing things. When there is nothing else to learn, integrate them in your own life. If you discover there is a need to improve something offer your help humbly, without imposing, without assuming. Look at others and your surroundings with respect because you are looking at yourself. Do not try to impose your ideas. You are a visitor, never allow yourself to feel too comfortable to lose desire to be careful, respectful or offer quality time to others. Practice active listening. Do not force anything or get affected by the detours along the way. Understand the strength and energy with which the circumstances move around you and enjoy the journey and the landscape. Seek to understand instead of imposing and always keep in mind your original objective: What is my contribution in the world? This develops self-projection and contribution and it will work at the capability and environment level, supporting the other changes you have established on higher levels.

Another exercise to activate the visitor attitude is to set a bell or alarm on your phone to ring every hour of the day (during awake times) for seven days. Every hour when the bell rings you will stop and think "I am alive, I still alive for another hour." Smile and be thankful for the extra time you received for being alive. Do this every hour (during day time) for seven days and something fundamental will happen to you. Eventually you will begging to invest your time on things that are really meaningful and important to you. We spend so much time on things that are irrelevant to us without realizing we are wasting our life. Millions of people die every day without having any health condition. They go to sleep and the next day they do not weak up. For some reason, we think is not going to happen to us. Being a visitor implies taking advantage of every minute of our lives, investing our time on the things that are more significant to us.

## Practice 4. Feed your self-approval

Learn to love and accept yourself just the way you are. You are just exactly where you need to be. You are who you are meant to be. There is no need for validation, but if any validation is deserved it should be your own.

Look at yourself in the mirror frequently and tell your image about those things which make you value yourself. Have compassion for yourself and acknowledge your efforts without criticizing your attempts or lack of apparent results. Pay attention to when you are looking for validation of others. Stop there and ask yourself, why am I waiting for validation? Where am I not validating myself? Recognize your small and big efforts. This develops self-projection competence and is working at the belief and identity levels.

## Practice 5. Look at others as if they were your mirror

Keep a small mirror in your pocket as a reminder that the other is your mirror. Develop your ability to be empathetic from the understanding that the other is your projection and, as such, is the mirror in which you reflect. Take advantage of this understanding by observing carefully so that you know yourself through the other and remember that what you reject from others is a side that you are rejecting of yourself. What you admire in others is a side of yourself that you do not allow yourself to exhibit or you think you lack, so you set both on the outside to be able to observe and transcend. The ultimate goal is to integrate everything in our selves and at the same time recognize us as part of the whole. Accept and practice that everything you see, every object, every situation you live means nothing more than what you decide it to be. It is your choice. Things alone are just things. They lack meaning. This develops self-projection and it works at the system level.

There is no magic formula that can transform something once and forever. We are energy in continuous movement and transformation like everything around us. There is nothing static in the universe and today's challenge will not be the challenge of tomorrow. Who I am today won't be the person of tomorrow. Besides, where would we be without new challenges? We would end up losing motivation and getting bored. Our brains would quickly age in the absence of stimuli. Challenges are what make us grow, evolve, and acknowledge who we really are.

What we can achieve through the practice of original intelligence and its awareness is that although the challenges change, the solution is always systemic, sustainable, effective and efficient through something we all know, but we have forgotten, internal coherence. Now your job is to remember and practice.

# ABSTRACT OR SUMMARY

I propose a new model of intelligence that involves remembering. An intelligence that has been given to us since before our birth when we were in coherence, which is the original intelligence. This new model is inspired on the discovery of the brain of the heart and its ability to create homeostasis, not only at a biological level but also on a mental, emotional and spiritual level.

I have described four personalities or ways of living that reflect the accentuated use of each brain. The oldest brain of the three, called the Reptilian Brain, is responsible for controlling the most vital functions of the body such as breathing, body temperature, and balance. This brain reflects our four most basic motivating or instinctive survival behaviors: feeding, fighting, escaping, and reproduction.

The reptilian lifestyle is rigid, basic, and compulsive. The reptilian personality seeks survival and satisfying our most basic needs. Generally, reptilian personalities act from one or more of these four motivators that are activated by traumatic or unresolved childhood experiences in which they have felt at risk, unprotected, abandoned, or rejected.

Above the reptilian brain, we have the limbic brain, which stores our emotions and memories. In it we find the amygdala, considered the basis of affective memory. Among the functions and motivations of the limbic brain are fear, anger, the love of our parents, social relations, and jealousy. The limbic lifestyle is intense, sensitive, and even dramatic. Everything can affect a person of negative limbic personality. All can be taken by heart, and this person can be spiteful, nervous, undecided, depressive and anxious because they feel frequently attacked by their environment or others. On the positive side, we can also find extremely emotionally sensitive people who feel empathy and easily connect with the emotions of others, but if they stay in this brain they will not be able to transcend their emotions.

Next, we have the neocortex or rational brain, which allows us to have awareness and control of emotions, while developing cognitive capacities such as memorization, concentration, self-reflection, problem solving, and the ability to choose the appropriate behavior. This is the conscious part of the person, both physiologically and emotionally. The rational way of life, as its name suggests, is calculated and even-tempered. A person with a rational personality is calculating, wants to find rational explanations to everything he or she sees or experiences, can be unbelieving, pragmatic, emotional repressive, abhor drama and, taken to the extreme, can be insensitive or short of empathy.

Then we have the fourth brain, the brain of the heart. It is the last to be discovered but the first that appears biologically. This brain is in charge of inhibiting or activating certain parts of the head brain according to the circumstances. It controls hormones and neurotransmitters, produces the ANF hormone or atrial natriuretic factor, which ensures the general balance of the body, or homeostasis. The heart also inhibits the production of the stress hormone and releases the love hormone called oxytocin. It sends messages not only to the brain of the head but to our whole body through the heart. The heart has the most potent electromagnetic field of all bodily organs, becoming 5,000 times more powerful than the electromagnetic field of the brain of the head. This extends around the body between two and four meters, depending on each person. This electromagnetic field changes according to our emotions since it also happens in our brain of the head when we harbor negative or positive thoughts. Emotions, like anger, fear, and stress, make this field lose coherence and order while emotions like love, compassion and joy keep the field in order and harmony.

The heart personality is compassionate, loving, breathes in harmony, feels part of a whole, does not judge, but seeks alternatives and solutions, looking for the positive side of things, is optimistic, cheerful and collaborative, takes responsibility for its actions. It is connected with its interior and its purpose of life and expresses it easily.

When we use one of our brains more than others it determines our way of life. The fourth brain, the brain of the heart, constitutes the source of our original intelligence, the opportunity to transcend our limitations of thoughts, beliefs, interpretations and its particular emotions.

We are not trying to get rid of any brain. Our intent is to find homeostasis and balance between the four brains and use them wisely. However, the brain of the heart is the catalyzer that best regulates the other brains and could significantly transform our way of living.

The original intelligence model has five components:

1. **Coherence**: Original or transpersonal state of our being that expresses an intelligence to maintain our wellbeing.
2. **Self-awareness:** Inner communication, level of attention and expression of visitor attitude, acknowledgment of our emotions, thoughts and self.

3. **Self-projection**: External communication, ability to connect and empathize, self-recognition through the other, ability to project ourselves to the world.
4. **Inspiration**: Learning desire, project and purpose of life, vital energy.
5. **Contribution**: Service gift or strength that I express to the world.

To remember and develop the original intelligence and its elements I have suggested five practices:

## Practice 1. Breathing and meditation

We must meditate focusing our attention on the present with each and every one of our senses, without judging anything as good or bad, right or wrong. Just appreciating and observing what is there provides openness, inner coherence, returns us to a zero state where everything starts again without past or future and the possibilities of everything increases. We have to take care of our vibratory environment, collaborate with others, altruistically help others to be happy, enjoy the little things in life in the present. This develops self-consciousness.

Practice focusing your attention on the area of the heart while breathing rhythmically and recreating feelings of compassion, love, fraternity, and equanimity. This helps to develop internal coherence and activates the brain of the heart.

## Practice 2. Cultivate silence

Cultivate silence, explore your interior in periods of solitude, contact with nature, contemplate in quietness how your thoughts pass as clouds that we let go until we find spaces between thoughts. There we will find silence. Cultivating silence helps us calm the chaotic dialogue and save energy. To achieve internal silence begins by practicing mindfulness. And in order to reach deeper levels of consciousness and silence practice transcendental meditation or any kind of meditation that focuses on cultivating inner silence. When you reach that point, ask yourself:

1. Who am I?
2. What do I want?
3. What is my purpose in life?
4. What am I thankful for?

Just ask the questions without preconceptions or looking for an immediate answer. Simply introduce the questions in the silence of your inner self and leave them there for your conscious mind to respond in the correct time and in ways you do not imagine. This practice develops self-awareness and inspiration.

## Practice 3. Take the visitor attitude

Practicing the attitude of visitor is a choice that we can make daily in any area of our life. Ask more than what you say and do it with curiosity and open mind to learn, cultivate curiosity towards others and their motivations. Look at others and your surroundings with respect because you are looking at yourself. Do not try to impose your ideas. You are a visitor, never allow yourself to feel too comfortable so you can lose the desire to be careful, respectful or offer quality time to others. Practice active listening. Do not force anything nor do you get affected by the detours along the way. Understand the strength and energy with which the circumstances move around you and enjoy the journey, seek to understand instead of imposing and always keep in mind your original objective. What is my contribution in the world? This develops self-projection and contribution.

## Practice 4. Feed self-acceptance.

Pay attention to when you are looking for validation of others. Stop there and ask why am I doing this? Why am I not validating myself? This develops self-projection competence.

## Practice 5. Look at other as if they were your mirror.

Keep a small mirror in your pocket as a reminder that the other is your mirror. Take advantage of this understanding by observing carefully so that you know yourself through the other and remember that what you reject from the other is a side that you are rejecting of yourself and what you admire of the other is a side of yourself that you do not allow yourself to exhibit or you think you lack and so you set both on the outside to be able to observe and transcend. The goal at the end is to integrate everything and at the same time identify ourselves as part of the whole.

# APPENDIX

- Daniel H. Pink. DRIVE The Surprising Truth About What Motivates Us. River head books, 2009
- Jonathan Haidt. The Righteous Mind: Why Good People Are Divided by Politics and Religion. Vintage, 2012
- Mary Helen Immordino-Yang. Emotions, Learning, and the Brain: Exploring the Educational Implications of Affective Neuroscience. W. W. Norton, Incorporated, 2015
- Abraham Maslow. Motivation and Personality. Harper & Row, 1954
- Daniel Goleman. Emotional Intelligence. Bantam Books, 1995
- Brené Brown. The Gifts of Imperfection: Let Go of Who You Think You're Supposed to Be and Embrace Who You Are. Hezelden, 2010
- Carl G. Jung. The Undiscovered Self, The Dilemma Of The Individual In Modern Society. New American Library, 2006
- Gredd Braden, Fractal Time, Sirio, 2019
- Helen Schucman. A Course in Miracles. Foundation for Inner Peace, 1976

- Hearth Math Institute. Hearthmath.org. Accessed September, 2018
- Annie Marquier. El Maestro Del Corazón. Luciérnaga, 2010
- Corbera Enric. El Observador En Bioneuroemoción. El Grano De Mostaza, 2018

Printed in the United States
By Bookmasters